ONE KOREA?

ONE KOREA?

Challenges and Prospects for Reunification

Edited by
THOMAS H. HENRIKSEN
and KYONGSOO LHO

HOOVER INSTITUTION PRESS
Stanford University
Stanford, California

Hoover Institution Press Publication No. 421

Copyright © 1994 by the Board of Trustees of the
Leland Stanford Junior University

First printing, 1994
00 99 98 97 96 95 94   9 8 7 6 5 4 3 2 1
First paperback printing, 1994
00 99 98   9 8 7 6 5 4 3

Manufactured in the United States of America

The paper used in this publication meets the minimum requirements
of American National Standard for Information Sciences—Permanence
of Paper for Printed Library Materials, ANSI Z39.48–1984. ⊗

Library of Congress Cataloging-in-Publication Data

One Korea? : challenges and prospects for reunification / edited by
Thomas H. Henriksen and Kyongsoo Lho.
        p.   cm.
    Includes bibliographical references and index.
    ISBN 0-8179-9291-X
    ISBN 0-8179-9292-8 (pbk.)
    1. Korean reunification question (1945–   )   I. Henriksen,
Thomas H.   II. Lho, Kyongsoo, 1954–   .
DS917.444.O54   1994
951.904—dc20   94-21480
                                           CIP

Contents

Acknowledgments

The chapters in this volume are based on presentations at a conference, "Korean Reunification: Challenges and Prospects in the 1990s," held at the Hoover Institution June 14–15, 1993. The conference was organized by Kyongsoo Lho and Thomas H. Henriksen as part of the Hoover Institution's Korean Studies Program. This program undertakes research, publications, conferences, seminars, and the interchange of experts to foster an exchange of information and viewpoints about the Korean peninsula and its economic and political relationship to the Pacific region and the United States.

The Hoover Institution is grateful for generous financial support from the Korea Foundation, which, in part, was instrumental in establishing the Korean Studies Program. We are particularly indebted to the generosity of the Korea Foundation's president, Son Chu-whan. The conference and this volume represent a portion of the program's activities.

The editors wish to express their thanks and appreciation to Hoover Institution director John Raisian for his personal encouragement and administrative support for the Korean Studies Program and its endeavors. We also want to thank Wendy Minkin for her help in coordinating the conference. For preparation of the manuscript for publication, we want to state our gratitude in particular to Karen Kenlay, Nancy Sharp, and Julie Wei. We are indebted to our colleague Ramon Myers, who read the manuscript and offered many thoughtful suggestions.

Thomas H. Henriksen

Kyongsoo Lho

Introduction

Thomas H. Henriksen
and Kyongsoo Lho

The end of the cold war sparked a chain of dramatic events around the world. The collapse of the Soviet Union and communism in Eastern Europe unsettled the western Eurasian land mass. New and newly independent nations emerged where the Red Army and communist parties had once prevailed. Political results occurred that few had prophesied as possible in their lifetimes. Soviet forces, for example, pulled out of most of East-Central Europe; the two Germanys unified; the Soviet Communist Party relinquished power. In Central Asia, breakaway states achieved a measure of self-determination even though their long-term independence seems fragile, given their economic difficulties and Moscow's clandestine activities. In Asia, Latin America, and Africa, ruling parties and political movements backed away from Marxist economies and Marxist visions. Instead, democracy and free market systems enjoyed a newfound vogue. Political divisions disappeared, as when the formerly Marxist South Yemen united with the traditionalist North Yemen.

A handful of communist relics remain. But even in those countries—China, Cuba, and North Korea—hard evidence points to change. China is experimenting with free market reforms; Cuba is in its economic death throes; North Korea is attempting to play a nuclear card and thereby wring concessions to salvage its massive economic failures. Those Marxist islands appear doomed. Nowhere do these sweeping political changes impinge more closely on intrastate relations than on the Korean peninsula, which has been divided since 1945. The death of North Korea's long-term leader, Kim Il Sung, makes the subject of possible unification all the more compelling.

The prospect of Korean unification has captivated Korea's peoples for decades. It has been the subject of study, speculation, books, and tentative planning by politicians, journalists, and professors. Scenarios, programs, and commission reports have set forth the conditions for reunification and predicted future challenges. Non-Koreans in foreign ministries, defense agencies, and policy centers have also conjectured on the impact that a reunited Korea would have on the East Asian geopolitical landscape. The post–cold war circumstances have given renewed life and reality to visions of a reunified Korea. The fusion of East and West Germany, whose former political configurations resemble the Korean entities, has brought the merging of North and South Korea into the realm of possibility. Although less well known, the South-North Yemeni recombination added another case study of a nation divided by ideology and conflict coming together through peaceful negotiation, though that union is now in jeopardy.

The above-mentioned and other ongoing changes presented the Hoover Institution with the opportunity to convene a conference and assess a possible end to the division in the Korean peninsula. Germany's reunification in particular served as a catalyst and possible prototype for a reunion of the Koreas. Pyongyang's announcement of its withdrawal from the nuclear Non-Proliferation Treaty in March 1993, however, added a new and significant dimension. The current nuclear standoff on the Korean peninsula could result in a catastrophe, a fact acknowledged by the Hoover conference participants. But many scenarios still exist for reunification.

The conference, entitled "Korean Reunification: Challenges and Prospects in the 1990s," brought together Korean, American, and European scholars June 14–15, 1993. Held a year before Kim Il Sung's death, the conference participants took into account his possible departure from the political stage in their presentations. The participants included policy specialists who differed over the prospects for unification and the magnitude of the problems that would follow. They did, however, share some common assumptions.

Most participants agreed that the difficulties and huge expense of German reunification raised caution flags against precipitously reuniting the Koreas. A sudden collapse of the North Korean regime would mean that the South Koreans would have to cope with a massive and immediate economic bailout to restore the industry, agriculture, and living standards of their Northern cousins. South Korea could also face a human tidal wave of North Koreans fleeing misery and hunger that could swamp the South, which would be unable to absorb, feed, or put to work hordes of destitute people.

The participants agreed that the optimal solution to North Korea's problems would be a slow-paced loosening of the totalitarian political grip, accompanied by a gradually expanding market economy before reunification. The North's deliberately developing political freedom and economic growth would facilitate a merger between the two countries on more equal terms, perhaps in some form of interim federated state. An abrupt collapse of the Pyongyang regime followed by civil turmoil would saddle South Korea with rehabilitating a strife-filled and failed state. The costs could be high in blood and treasure.

Each conference presentation reflected the changed global circumstances, the German case study in reunification, and the impact on possible Korean reunification. The participants estimated the challenges faced by Pyongyang, examined various options for North Korea, envisioned possible reunification scenarios, and anticipated benefits as well as problems from the reuniting process and afterward. Most took into account Pyongyang's nuclear program and gauged its impact on unification as well as on regional geopolitical relationships.

Korea Foundation president Son Chu-whan opened the conference with an overview of the changed world circumstances and changing conditions on the Korean peninsula. In his remarks, "Korean Unification Ahead: Hopeful but Treacherous Road," he viewed the main barrier to Korean reunification as being the cold war stance of Pyongyang. But he also noted the great distrust the North and South have of one another.

The older generation of South Koreans, though distrustful, yearns for reunification. The younger generation, however, has no memory of a war or of a united Korea. Those young people have created a new culture and new values that may distance them even further from North Korea. According to Son, the South Korean government, aware that delay may make reunification remote, took several steps in the 1980s to improve relations with the North. In 1991 and 1992, the Agreement on Reconciliation and the Joint Declaration on Denuclearization were signed by North and South. The South Korean goal has been to reestablish national homogeneity through active cultural and economic exchanges, reciprocal television broadcasts, and interchange of people to ease reunification.

In Son's view, North Korea fears that opening its doors would lead to political collapse, as in the case of other Marxist-Leninist countries. But the Republic of Korea has tried to allay the North's fears by proposing a gradual approach to mutual economic exchange and cooperation, with the South providing capital and technology and the North, labor and resources. Such cooperation would contribute to stability in Northeast Asia and minimize unification costs in the long run. Son said, however, that the North must change its fundamental attitudes and accept inspections by the International

Atomic Energy Agency. The South successfully made the transition to democracy with the election of Kim Young-sam. But during the same period,
the North has remained in the total control of Kim Il Sung, who appears
bent on passing this power to his son for a continuation of absolute rule. To
Son, this hereditary autocracy would perpetuate the barriers to reunification.

In the first chapter of this book, "North Korea: Reform, Muddling
through, or Collapse?" Nicholas Eberstadt looks at Pyongyang's options.
As the oldest existing communist state, Eberstadt sees North Korea's longevity as a measure of its political strength and holds that Pyongyang's brand
of pragmatism has been underestimated. But changes since 1989, particularly the loss of aid from communist regimes first in Eastern Europe and
then the former Soviet Union, have pushed the North Korean economy into
a nosedive.

Eberstadt contends that North Korea faces three scenarios: reform,
muddling through, and collapse. Recent economic reforms, such as the 1984
Joint Venture Law, the Law on Free Economic and Trade Zones, the multi-
nation Tumen development project, the Foreign Direct Investment Law, and
the Foreign Investment Law, are halfhearted and peripheral attempts at
reform that have not touched the fundamental problems, such as central
planning, the extraordinary expenditure on the military, and the lack of
information flow and scientific contacts. There is no sign that Kim Il Sung
will risk basic reform. Muddling through also will not work; Pyongyang's
only hope is the political instability of the South Korean system. Eberstadt
concludes that this scenario holds little prospect of delivering the North
from its plight. Since 1987, two open, competitive, mass presidential cam-
paigns have taken place in South Korea, and the South Korean polity is
gaining strength, steadily moving toward cooperation, coalition building,
and consensus seeking.

To Eberstadt, the remaining alternative is a North Korean collapse, and,
indeed, North Korea appears headed toward an implosion. As a last act of
desperation, North Korea may use its nuclear weaponry as an all-purpose
instrument of diplomacy to ensure its regime and leadership. Pyongyang
employs the nuclear threat to bargain for a successful transition of leadership
from father to son or to gain economic assistance. As long as nuclear weapons serve as a means of blackmail, North Korea will surely not give up its
nuclear weapons program, no matter what agreements Pyongyang may sign.

Korean reunification will be expensive, like Germany's, entailing subsidies and pensions to individuals and firms and a massive investment to
modernize North Korea's economy. According to Aidan Foster-Carter, however, Korea is now far more able to influence its fate than it had been in the
1890s or 1940s. Reunification could be gradual and evolutionary, he writes,
or sudden and revolutionary, following North Korea's collapse and absorption into South Korea.

In his chapter, "Sociopolitical Realities of Reuniting a Divided Nation," Foster-Carter holds that the "collapsist" scenario is the most plausible because present economic contraction, about 5 percent annually, can only end in implosion, leading to the overthrow of the regime and popular demand for immediate integration. Kim Il Sung refused to institute economic reforms lest perestroika lead inevitably to glasnost.

Sociologically, North Korea is not sui generis, not unique, despite the claims of *juche* (self-reliance), according to Foster-Carter. Whether socialist, communist, or Stalinist, it cannot avoid the fate of others of its ilk. In Foster-Carter's opinion, we can infer the sociologic of reunification from empirical data ranging from Eberstadt's pioneering work on population and labor force data to Kim Il Sung's own writings. North Koreans are economically and socially conservative; two-thirds to three-quarters of them are classified by the Kim government as being "wavering" or "hostile" to the government, hence subject to privation and discrimination. Most North Koreans have nothing to lose but their chains.

Reunification needs to be well managed, learning from the German and Yemen experiences. But South Korea already possesses policy skills for yoking state and capital for national unification. Problems in reunification include the reunion of separated families, influx control at the demilitarized zone (DMZ), financial responsibility for immigrants from the North, claims in the North, and the role of the churches as mediators in civil society. There are other problems. Should the DMZ be maintained? Should North Korea be administered from Seoul or Pyongyang? How should the Northern labor force be trimmed? How would such reductions affect workers, especially women workers? What should be done with the huge Northern army?

Although Koreans yearned for fusion long before German union, the prohibitive cost of German reunification has given Koreans second thoughts about quick reunification. In his essay, Jongryn Mo posits that South Korea now favors a multistage reunification process, either a negotiated merger or a one-sided absorption, as in the German case. A gradual, negotiated merger would require that North Korea implement a far-reaching reform program. But because that is unlikely, Mo argues, the North will probably collapse, and South Korea will initiate a one-sided absorption to avoid anarchy.

Given the strong possibility of one-sided absorption, Korea must draw proper lessons from the German experience. In Mo's essay, "German Lessons for Managing the Economic Cost of Korean Reunification," he states that South Korea can successfully manage Korean reunification by learning from the mistakes of Chancellor Helmut Kohl's government. The first lesson is that Germany's reunification took place too quickly. The German border was opened in November 1989; in February 1990, Kohl reversed his gradualist ten-point plan in favor of immediate reunification. Economic union took place in July 1990, and full reunification occurred in October 1990.

(Because Kohl's government was not secure, immediate reunification was a means of gaining electoral support.) Second, when wages in East Germany rose rapidly after reunification, owing mainly to union bargaining power, the government pursued a traditional hands-off wage policy and did not intervene until 1993. Third, the slow pace of privatizing state-run companies hampered the recovery of the German economy. One main reason for slow privatization was the decision to restore property rights to former owners, causing disputes over property rights. Thus the Treuhand (the state agency) did not have clear title to all the holdings it aimed to privatize.

Mo then turns to the Korean situation and discusses how to avoid each of these mistakes. The South Korean regime is politically secure and therefore need not bow to political pressures for a "big bang" approach to reunification. However, Korea should also examine what Germany did right.

Although recombining North and South Korea may be sui generis, two previous examples could provide helpful comparisons, according to Thomas H. Henriksen's essay, "Political Leadership, Vision, and Korean Reunification." German reunification was an "acquisition," and Yemeni reunification, a "merger." One thing North Korea and East Germany have in common is communism. In other ways, the German and the Korean cases are very different. East Germany's seventeen million people were about one-fourth of West Germany's sixty million, while North Korea's twenty-one million constitute half of South Korea's forty-three million. The two Germanys had experienced peaceful coexistence and growing economic cooperation, but North Korea forbids interstate travel and reciprocal trade or communication between separated families. East Germany had sympathizers and proponents in the West who touted its welfare system, its reputed absence of crime, and so forth. In contrast, North Korea's hermetic isolation and Stalinist terror have won little sympathy from the West. The Germans lack a strong sense of national identity, while the Koreans' sense of national identity is strong.

The Yemeni reunification defied stereotypes of the Middle East, where bloody conflicts, not cooperation, characterize politics. Henriksen observes that Yemen's reunification was gradual and peaceful, carefully planned and executed. Armed conflict between the North and South ended in 1982, followed by economic, sociopolitical, and military steps toward cooperation. In 1986, the Marxist government in the South collapsed after bloody turmoil; the North meanwhile had introduced multiparty democracy. After two years, both sides withdrew military forces from the borderlands. The two sides agreed on the free movement of citizens and goods over the border and also linked their two electric power grids. A joint committee was convened in 1989 to lay the groundwork for reunification, and a joint constitution was ratified. The key political positions in the new government were divided between the two parties, and the devoutly Islamic North and the secular

Marxist South were reunited in a phased, peaceful manner. Tensions between the two parties remained after reunification, however, threatening to break up the government at the end of 1993. Civil war between North and South did break out in May 1994, demonstrating that even a reunification process as exemplary as that of Yemen does not guarantee continuing reconciliation. Still, the German and Yemeni reunifications offer lessons and examples for Koreans to study.

Just as the external threat of Saudi Arabia helped Yemenis reunite, so the presence of powerful neighbors—China, Japan, and Russia—may promote Korean reunification. But promoting the transition from totalitarianism to political pluralism and free markets calls for leadership and political vision. Models of such leadership are West Germany's Helmut Kohl, North Yemen president Ali Abdullah Salih, and America's Abraham Lincoln, who called for reconciliation in uniting the North and South. Although events in the United States during the 1860s are not usually associated with Korea or postcommunist reunification, a few parallels are worthy of attention. Lincoln's assassination in the final days of the American Civil War created many problems during the Reconstruction era that lengthened and embittered the reunification of the American North and South. Carpetbaggers and scalawags sowed hatred and divisiveness among Southerners that lasted for many decades. To avoid similar pitfalls, Henriksen suggests that South Korean leaders set up reconciliation mechanisms for government, political parties, corporations, trade unions, universities, schools, churches, the military, and other institutions alike. They should also look closely at the societal ills that befell East Germany and Russia after the cold war as well as the American South during the Reconstruction era, with the aim of avoiding or lessening similar problems after Korean reunification.

According to Man Won Jee, in his essay "Forging a Common Security View: Prospects for Arms Control in Korea," neither North Korean nor South Korean leaders have been sincere in their reunification policies. Ever since the Sixth Republic, the South Korean government's North Korean policy has aimed at reunification through reform in Pyongyang, economic assistance to North Korea, and settling the nuclear issue. North Korea, in contrast, has encouraged its citizens to believe that they must liberate their fellow South Koreans from poverty and hunger. Each side has used the emotional issue of reunification as a tool to justify its policies, control its populations, and maintain political power.

When Pyongyang's proposal for a Democratic Confederal Republic of Koryo won attention internationally and in South Korea, the South's leaders, from Chun Doo Hwan to Roh Tae Woo, began using their own National Reunification Board, Advisory Body for Peaceful Reunification, and other groups primarily as tools to maintain themselves in office. The South's Korea

National Community Unification Formula, in Jee's judgment, is deliberately obscure, having neither a clear ideology nor a clear objective.

South Koreans do not want the financial burden of a Northern collapse and reunification through absorption. Nor do they want to force reform on the North, as precipitous reform will bring about glasnost and collapse. The only realistic way to solve the problem is for North and South to abandon their reunification efforts and coexist with each other without interference, as South Korea has coexisted with Japan, resulting in mutual prosperity. This would allow the ending of the costly arms race and the diplomatic competition and would permit mutually beneficial economic cooperation. In Jee's opinion, South Korea must clarify its reunification policy and shift from confrontation to peaceful coexistence, from glasnost and reunification to peaceful coexistence and arms reduction.

The two main requisites for peaceful coexistence are reducing the military and eliminating suspicion, Jee writes. To eliminate suspicion, there needs to be joint control of the armed forces, with a command structure similar to that of the North Atlantic Treaty Organization (NATO), he maintains. To address the nuclear issue, observers must understand why North Korea feels that nuclear arms are necessary. The North Korean economy is collapsing, and nuclear weapons are the North's last negotiating card. The North has also fallen behind the South in conventional weapons: the South has spent billions over the past several years for F-16s, submarines, and other weapons, while the North has not been able to purchase a single new fighter plane. Washington, according to Jee, should abandon international mechanisms to deal with the nuclear issue and view the issue as an internal problem.

U.S. military forces in Korea have served as a deterrent against war in the peninsula, and Pyongyang must understand that any attempt to start a war will end badly. Learning from the Iraq war experience, South Korea, Jee declares, must replace its large military force with a smaller but more technologically advanced one. Such a reduction should not be based on a negotiated mutual reduction with the North but on Seoul's economic ability. Seoul's arms reduction initiative, Jee predicts, will open Pyongyang's eyes to the seriousness of economic warfare, shift its attention from military to commercial issues, and encourage economic reform and eventual glasnost. Military reduction will shift more than 300,000 of South Korea's top-quality workforce to the commercial sector, producing a total gain of one trillion won in South Korea's gross national product.

Until now, Pyongyang has taken the leading role in advocating mutual arms reductions, Jee notes, and it is South Korea's military that has used the threat of the North to oppose military cutbacks. The motives of South

Korea's military in opposing arms reduction, Jee asserts, are to maintain the power and prestige of their high-ranking officers.

With the end of the cold war, Seoul's normalization of relations with Moscow and Beijing has helped isolate North Korea, according to Tetsuya Kataoka's essay, "Scratching an Old Wound: Japan's Perspective on Korea and Its Unification." Pyongyang's withdrawal from the Non-Proliferation Treaty (NPT) in March 1993, however, was a brilliant political stroke. By playing on President Bill Clinton's fear of nuclear proliferation and his unwillingness to go to war, Pyongyang forced Washington to deal with North Korea from a new perspective. The specter of war also forced China to be North Korea's great rearguard once again, Kataoka observes. Clinton's willingness to talk to avoid war may well pave the way to Washington's recognition of North Korea, which may lead to Tokyo's recognition of North Korea—the ultimate objective of Kim Il Sung's nuclear initiative. In Kataoka's opinion, even if Kim had returned to the NPT and agreed to bilateral inspection, he would probably still have used loopholes to build nuclear weapons. Had that occurred, the position of U.S. troops in Korea would be untenable and they might be withdrawn. John M. Deutsche (former undersecretary of defense for acquisition and technology) has proposed that Japan arm itself with a network of Patriot missiles to counter North Korea's improved Scud missile, Rodong 1, and its successors.

All the wars in East Asia fought by Japan in modern times, according to Kataoka, have also involved Korea, whose security is necessary to Japan's safety. Japan went to war with the United States when it demanded, in the Hull Note, that Japan withdraw from Manchuria, adjacent to Korea. Later, during the Korean War, many Americans, especially Republicans, became convinced that "we fought the wrong enemy." When John Foster Dulles asked Prime Minister Shigeru Yoshida to send Japanese troops to fight in Korea, Yoshida refused because Japan had all along fought "the right enemy," the Russian and Chinese Communists. Yet Franklin Roosevelt's America had looked on Japan as the aggressor. The Korean and Vietnam Wars are "directly traceable to the destruction of the regional order that Japan had built," in Kataoka's judgment. The United States has striven to liberate the Korean people from the yoke of Japanese colonialism and encouraged anticolonial sentiment in South Korea. In Kataoka's opinion, America also created the antimilitarist regime in Japan and thus placed itself in the middle of an alliance system. Washington has recently egged on Korean-Japanese hostility, a by-product of the hub-and-spoke arrangement in Asia whereby America has made itself the center of bilateral agreements with Asian nations.

According to Kataoka, the Clinton administration took over Dean Acheson's original assumption that Japan was separable from Korea in foreign policy. But now, with Pax Americana in decline, can the United States, Japan, and the Korean people afford a withdrawal of U.S. forces from South Korea? A retreat of the U.S. forces would nullify the U.S.–Republic of Korea (ROK) and U.S.-Japan defense pacts (made to defend Korea), which will advance China's influence. If Tokyo were to revive militarism, on the one hand, Japan may offset China's military power. On the other hand, Japan might become Finlandized, and then South Korea would be isolated. Then China would help Pyongyang to unify Korea on its own terms, paving the way for a greater East Asian coprosperity zone under Chinese hegemony, Kataoka maintains.

Assuming Korean reunification will occur and that a reunified Korea will be administered from Seoul, Edward A. Olsen asserts that the United States must assess the implications of reunification on the U.S.-Korean alliance. The U.S. involvement in the Korean War was part of a larger struggle to enforce containment in an emerging global war. Washington's participation occurred in response to a perceived threat to Japan and America's Pacific, symbolized in Japan. The inter-Korean border became a parallel to the NATO–Warsaw Pact frontline, according to Olsen's essay, "Korea's Reunification: Implications for the U.S.-ROK Alliance."

The ROK has moved from being a client state and U.S. protégé to being a junior partner in regional security affairs, Olsen argues. As a client state, it was transformed societally and geopolitically through U.S. aid, investment, and technology and through membership in the diplomatic and economic network of the Western alliance. South Korea has furthermore turned into an economic partner and competitor; with the end of the cold war, it has assumed greater diplomatic and political independence.

South Korea, in Olsen's opinion, is far more prepared for reunification than the United States, which has yet to adjust to the implications of the end of the cold war for Asia or to devise an Asia-focused post–cold war policy. According to Olsen, Americans should methodically prepare for Korean unification, drawing lessons from Germany and examining the financial, political, and security implications. The United States should look at the implications for Korea's relations with China, Russia, and Japan and also at those between China, Russia, Japan, and the United States. Americans should not embark on an alliance with a unified Korea without examining whether this will be perceived as a threat by China, Russia, or Japan. Olsen, however, also cites the argument of Chalmers Johnson, who suggests that a long-term alliance with unified Korea might keep China and Japan off balance. According to this view, American ties with Korea, Vietnam, and the Association of Southeast Asian Nations would be part of an emerging larger Asian balance of power against China and Japan.

The cold war is over in most parts of the globe. Yet the ideological standoff still haunts the Korean peninsula with the prospect of war, even nuclear calamity. The contributors to this volume understand the role of chance in history—that the current deadlock in arms control negotiations might conceivably give way to nuclear catastrophe. Despite the threat of hostilities, however, policy makers and scholars alike must envision a reunified Korea. The two Koreas, the contributors believe, must seek to avoid those problems associated with the collapse of communism in East-Central Europe and elsewhere in unifying their country into one Korea.

1

North Korea: Reform, Muddling through, or Collapse?

Nicholas Eberstadt

From its founding in 1948 to the present day, the Democratic People's Republic of Korea (DPRK) has pursued a foreign policy distinct among nations in the modern world for its high and seemingly permanent state of tension. The observation that the DPRK's relations with the international community are currently in a state of crisis may therefore seem unexceptional. Yet even for a government accustomed to international confrontation, the level of tension in North Korean external relations today is extraordinary. Indeed, as Pyongyang pursues its nuclear showdown against virtually all other governments of the contemporary world, it approaches a terrain of extreme and incalculable danger—a terrain it has entered only once before, in 1950, when its invasion of South Korea prompted a United Nations police action that was to become a devastating three-year multinational war.

By comparison with the events that unleashed the Korean War, the ongoing drama of North Korea's quest to develop atomic weaponry appears plodding and civil. North Korea's now famous March 12, 1993, announcement of its formal intention to withdraw from the Non-Proliferation Treaty (NPT)—the proximate focus of today's international alarms—came as the culmination of more than a year of detailed discussions and methodical deliberations involving the Republic of Korea (ROK), the United States, the International Atomic Energy Agency (IAEA), and other parties. Since the March 12 announcement, moreover, Pyongyang has actively promoted talks with foreign governments over possible formulas or procedures for defusing the crisis it has ignited. Pyongyang furthermore adhered to the letter of international law in acknowledging its obligation to remain a member of the NPT for ninety days after tendering its withdrawal. And in announcing a "temporary suspension" of its NPT withdrawal on June 11, 1993—the day before its scheduled departure from the treaty—North Korea chose continuing discussions over immediate conflict.

These forensics cannot conceal the grave situation that is developing, however. North Korea's March 1993 NPT announcement came in the wake of a series of meetings in which IAEA officials presented evidence that the DPRK, in violation of its duties by that treaty, not only had been producing nuclear materials that could be used for atomic weapons but had attempted to deceive IAEA inspectors about those efforts. The NPT announcement, far from being an isolated sore point, seems instead emblematic of a new turn toward international confrontation, even against erstwhile allies. Early in 1993, for example, North Korea expelled the Czech representatives of the Neutral Nations Supervisory Commission (NNSC) from its territory.[1] This delegation had been authorized to observe the demilitarized zone cease-fire since 1953. On March 8—four days before the NPT announcement—the North Korean People's Army (KPA) was ordered to "enter into a semistate of war" by its supreme commander, Kim Jong Il.[2] In April, unconfirmed reports of border incidents in which North Korean troops allegedly shot and killed Chinese nationals circulated in the international press.[3] That same month, North Korea's media raised the prospect of "an unpredictable grave consequence from which Japan will never escape" should Tokyo continue to press the North Korean nuclear issue.[4] In June, foreign diplomats confirmed reports that Pyongyang had ceased issuing entry visas, and rumors suggested that North Korean authorities were thinking about ordering all foreigners, except accredited diplomats, out of the country.[5] In July, the Russian government lodged an official protest after a Russian family was attacked on the streets of Nampo; it advised that "for the time being . . . the safety of Russian people [in North Korea] cannot be guaranteed."[6] Individually, these events or accounts might be downplayed or discounted. Taken together, they are consistent with North Korea's relations with the outside world entering a critical new phase—an impression starkly reinforced by North Korea's lone dissent in the 140 to 1 vote in the United Nations in November 1993 on international atomic inspections for the DPRK.[7]

The perilous implications of a completed North Korean nuclear weapons program hardly require emphasis. A North Korean nuclear capability would radically alter the nature of the security threat to South Korea and its allies; it would add to an accelerating arms race throughout East Asia; and it would reduce prospects of dissuading conventionally armed, revisionist states from fulfilling whatever nuclear ambitions they might entertain. International objections to North Korea's atomic quest, in short, could not be more solidly grounded. Yet in the commotion over these objections, a separate and only slightly less troubling issue has been obscured: If this nuclear crisis were somehow completely resolved today—indeed, if the DPRK were to dismantle all existing atomic facilities and forswear nuclear research forever—it would still pose an enormous and growing problem to the international community.

Even without nuclear weapons, North Korea possesses a massive and aggressively disposed military machine. This country of slightly more than twenty million people fields an army that is, in the estimate of the London International Institute of Strategic Studies (IISS), the fifth largest in the world today, with at least 1.1 million men under arms.[8] North Korea's ratio of troops to total population appears to be the highest for any country in the post–cold war era, rivaling the ratios achieved by the combatant powers of World War II during their drives for total mobilization.[9] Described in the early 1970s as "perhaps the most highly militarized society in the world today," the DPRK has, in the intervening decades, continued to relentlessly build up its forces and their capabilities.[10]

That the KPA is poised to inflict terrible destruction on South Korea is well understood. Less appreciated is the fact that it could do so without an invasion. Forward-deployed KPA artillery, for example, have the industrial metropolis of Seoul well within their range. Nor is South Korea the only North Korean neighbor hypothetically in harm's way. North Korea's new No Dong missile reportedly has a range of 1,000 kilometers.[11] Such population centers as Kyoto, Beijing, and Khabarovsk all lie less than 1,000 kilometers from North Korean territory. This circumstance in and of itself would be expected to sharpen Russian, Chinese, and Japanese interests in stable and predictable North Korean behavior. Recent reports that the KPA "is capable of producing and employing chemical weapons that virtually all fire-support systems in its inventory could deliver" can only intensify their concerns about the reliability of North Korean decision making.[12]

Unfortunately for all Northeast Asia, this fearsomely armed and tensely coiled state is moving, day by day, toward a juncture whose outcome is completely unpredictable but whose results could include instability and turmoil. The DPRK inexorably reached a leadership transition, the first and only in its history. The transition has been dictated not by political considerations but by biological realities: Kim Il Sung, the supreme political presence in North Korea since the founding of the state, is now dead. The designated heir is his firstborn son, KPA supreme commander Kim Jong Il, a reclusive middle-aged man about whom little is known but whose writings and speeches have revolved around such themes as the inspirational properties of the state cinema and the DPRK's officially espoused *juche* (often translated as "self-reliance") thought.

The likelihood of stable and predictable state behavior during the intended transition, and thereafter, has not been enhanced by the turn of events during 1988–1994. Since 1988, the North Korean economy has moved from stagnation to decline. Pyongyang has lost nearly all its international allies. The attraction exerted by the peninsular presence of the rival South Korean state has dramatically increased with the success of Seoul's experiment in political liberalization.

The argument may be advanced that a tense and delicate international posture for North Korea was foreordained—as it would have been for any small country that fiercely maintained its independence in the face of looming hegemons. In deference to that argument, one must concede that the DPRK has indeed suffered for its location. No small country seeking a spot on the map would of its own volition select precisely the place where the spheres of influence of the four great powers of the Pacific (Russia, China, Japan, and the United States) collide. But this structural argument neglects an essential point. No matter how star-crossed its geography, North Korea's current problems with the international community devolve directly from its own policy choices and actions. It is not easy to alienate or antagonize all the great powers in one's vicinity simultaneously, especially as tensions among those powers are on the wane. Yet this is exactly what the DPRK has succeeded in doing.

Paradoxically, to conclude that North Korea's current international problems are of its own making is to perceive some hope for the future. If the DPRK has created the perimeter of tension now surrounding it, the key to a regional, and international, détente lies in the hands of the North Korean government. Confidence and stability in North Korea's dealings with other governments can accrue only if the DPRK begins to act like other states.

Will the North Korean state emerge from its present international crisis and embark on a path toward normalcy in its international relations? More specifically, can that state, as it is presently constituted, open the door to détente with the rest of the world? Let us consider those questions in terms of the demonstrated strengths and capabilities of the existing regime, the pressures facing that state today, and the alternative adjustments to those pressures that would unfold through the mediating mechanism of the North Korean political system.

Unappreciated Accomplishments

North Korea's particular interpretation of socialism opens the DPRK to caricature abroad. The suffocating cult of personality for father and son, the clumsy but obsessive effort to control all information entering, circulating within, and leaving the country, the crude racialism and xenophobia, and the relentless drive to eliminate all private space from daily life present a bizarre and unappealing public face. However, it is easy to misassess—and to underestimate—the strengths of the state that wears the mask.

The capabilities of that government and its leadership are indirectly indicated by their longevity. The DPRK, after all, is today's oldest standing communist state. By the same token, Kim Il Sung was the contemporary world's longest-seated ruler, enjoying a tenure in office that has stretched over forty-five years. For a less idiosyncratic regime, such features of governance would be recognized as trappings of a certain kind of success.

Why has the DPRK survived when so many other communist regimes have perished in recent years? There is no simple answer. Yet striking, and arguably significant, differences separate North Korea's history and performance from the history and performance of other communist states. Of all Asia's state-imposed experiments in agricultural collectivization, only North Korea's did not result in famine. Similarly, North Korea may have borrowed the symbols and rhetoric of Mao's Great Leap Forward, but it avoided the reckless policies of that campaign—policies that brought on a collapse of China's industrial base that required years of undoing and repair.

Indeed, North Korea is probably the only communist state that has ever economically outperformed the capitalist rival against which it could most reasonably be compared. For roughly a quarter of a century—from the late 1940s through the early 1970s—North Korea's per capita gross national product (GNP), in the estimate of both Seoul and Washington, was higher than South Korea's.[13] By these reckonings, North Korea relinquished its lead only after the South Korean growth explosion had been under way for a decade.

Such results did not occur in a vacuum. On the contrary, they can be associated with abiding themes in Kim Il Sung's economic speeches and writings. To be sure, many of the great leader's pronouncements on economic affairs are utopian, exhortatory, and essentially coercive in nature. But another tendency has always been evident, a basic common sense about financial matters, such as that peasants and laborers will work harder and better if they are paid more, that prices of goods should be related to their quality, and that shortages can be eliminated, and supply enhanced, by seeking the price level at which transactions clear.[14] This is, of course, only a single strand of thought within a mesh of economic doctrine and dogma. One would be hard-pressed, however, to identify comparable quotations for party leaders from the erstwhile Soviet bloc.

If North Korean economic policy has been tempered over the decades by an unexpected element of pragmatism, its administrative decisions likewise reveal a practicality not immediately suggested by the regime's harsh and seemingly impulsive external declamations. That practicality is exemplified in the career of the current chief of the KPA General Staff, General Choi Kwang. In the late 1960s, Choi fell victim to a purge.[15] Directly accused by the great leader of undermining the country's military readiness and jeopardizing its national security, he completely disappeared from sight. For nearly a decade nothing was heard of him. Then, in 1977, he quietly reappeared and commenced a steady ascent. Today he directs the most important organization within the most important organization in the North Korean government. Such a rehabilitation would have been inconceivable in Stalin's Russia—or, for that matter, in any regime where Stalin was still viewed with official favor. Choi Kwang's fate, however, is indicative of a long-standing tendency in North Korea's politics to be sparing with potential assets that may prove useful to the regime at some future date.[16]

A final aspect of the North Korean interpretation of socialism deserves mention. The extraordinary concentration of power at the pinnacle of the North Korean hierarchy—more or less in the hands of two men—has been widely discussed (and ridiculed) overseas. What is less noticed is that the vanguard party these two men direct is a mass party as well. More than three million North Korean adults are said to be members of the Korea Workers' Party (KWP)—a figure that works out to roughly one adult in five.[17] Put another way, the country has enough party members that, in theory, every second North Korean household could contain one. Unlike most other Marxist-Leninist parties, which have typically attempted to maintain the elite status of the party by restricting membership to a small portion of the overall population, the KWP, from its earliest days, demonstrated its interest in developing a wide and deep cadre of operatives.[18] This broad base permits the North Korean party leadership to exercise ambitious and far-reaching control over the actions of its citizens at the local level.

By the criteria of liberal political theory, North Korean governance is a grotesque failure. But those criteria are irrelevant to North Korea's leadership, which judges its experiment in governance against a different set of standards. By those standards, North Korea has succeeded in developing a military force appropriate for a great power. It has erected and maintained a monolithic political order. No centers of authority exist apart from party and state, and within state and party there has been no challenge to Kim Il Sung's absolute mastery for a quarter of a century. The entire North Korean citizenry, by all external indications, behave as if they are unreservedly loyal to, enthusiastic about, and grateful for the nature of the rule that they experience. Not least important, those communist states that publicly criticized the DPRK's style of socialism have themselves vanished from the stage of history. Given this perspective, the North Korean leadership may perhaps be excused if it looks back at the country's record with a certain satisfaction and looks toward today's menacing developments with an air of confidence.

Mounting Economic Difficulties

Economic imbalances and structural distortions in the society do not seem to upset the North Korean leaders. They have, after all, presided over and intensified them. Nevertheless, these imbalances and distortions have reached a point where they should worry decision makers in the DPRK, for they now interfere with a prime objective of state, the augmenting of power by the regime.

Central to the dilemma is the KPA. This indispensable instrument of North Korean statecraft is valued in proportion to its size, but its size is now an insuperable burden for the economy that must support it. Manpower figures tell the story. By the late 1980s, noncivilian males accounted for fully a fifth of North Korea's men of working age.[19] Although North Korea's soldiers episodically engage in farming, construction, and the like, they are basically nonproductive workers who must draw sustenance and matériel from other sectors to perform their assigned tasks. Their immediate drag on the economy is substantial. But the growth of the KPA forestalls economic growth in other ways. Given North Korea's fertility trends and its government policies, there is no more surplus labor in the country. To satisfy its thirst for evermore inductees, the army must deprive state enterprises and universities of their recruits. In this institutional competition, the KPA's success in amassing its troop base undercuts training and productivity for the workforce as a whole. It is hardly a coincidence that North Korea's economic troubles began manifesting themselves in the early 1970s, exactly when the current tendency toward military buildup accelerated.

Just as North Korea's military has been abnormally expanded, so its consumer sector has been artificially compressed. Even by communist standards, North Korea's policies toward the consumer have always been severe. By one Western estimate, for example, the share of consumption in the North Korean economy in the 1950s was about twenty points lower than in the Soviet Union.[20] Since then, however, it appears that the share of output claimed by the consumer has been even further suppressed. Personal consumption expenditures, for example, are today an almost peripheral item in the North Korean economy. Rough calculations suggest that wages and salaries amount to no more than 15–25 percent of the nation's output.[21] Much of the population's consumption package is allocated directly to the household by the state, outside retail channels. Although it may seem convenient in the first instance for central planners to disconnect the preferences and desires of consumers from the workings of their planned economy, that separation imposes a variety of economic costs. Such austerity may affect human capital and thus the potential for augmenting growth. It cannot help but affect the motivation of the workforce. And by decommissioning price signals in the area where they were most likely to function well (at least under socialism)—the household—the North Korean government inadvertently increased the chances that waste would not be recognized or misallocations corrected.

Ever-increasing misallocation and waste, for their part, have been all but ordained by the thrust of North Korean central planning for a full generation. Civilian technocrats charged with enhancing the efficiency and productivity of the DPRK national economy seem to have suffered two complications in the early 1970s. First, the State Planning Commission was reportedly deprived of access to information about North Korea's huge and growing military economy, leaving technocrats in the dark about much of the overall economy they were expected to rationalize.[22] Second, the statistical blackout imposed on official DPRK publications and media was apparently accompanied by mounting pressures to politicize and inflate internally circulated production figures. By 1990, statistics officials in the DPRK joked that they were dealing in "rubber statistics."[23] In effect, the DPRK leadership, in Wolfgang Stolper's memorable phrase, had been reduced to "planning without facts."[24] This may help explain why the regime, when it was increasingly hard-pressed, embraced so many projects of questionable economic merit but extraordinary reported expense. (According to official sources, for example, the West Sea Gate Lock cost US $4 billion to complete; preparations for the 1989 Thirteenth World Youth Festival, including the necessary face-lift for Pyongyang, were said to cost US $4.7 billion.)[25]

Finally, the regime's muscular and unceasing activity in indoctrination and information control has strangled scientific and technological innovation in the DPRK. Officially, of course, North Korea has promoted "technical revolution" as a goal of the state (it is one of the three revolutions explicitly enumerated in a campaign that has been in motion for two decades). But North Korean scientists and intellectuals are expected to achieve their breakthroughs without knowledge or discretion or time to learn. (The curriculum in Kim Il Sung University is indicative of the broader situation.

As early as the 1970s students were spending nearly two-thirds of their course hours studying *juche,* Kim Il Sung thought, and other political topics, irrespective of their field of specialization.)[26] All but shut off from international contact and exchange, shielded from the outside world's information revolution, North Korea has become a research backwater, lagging behind in virtually all fields of inquiry. (Not even the North Korean nuclear drive—the enormously expensive program to replicate an American project completed half a century ago—contradicts this generalization.) By the early 1990s, in fact, North Korea was apparently the only country in Northeast Asia incapable of producing the microchip.[27] Such technological obsolescence not only limits the possibilities for economic development but undercuts the effectiveness of a military force that could be exposed to high-precision weapons and other advanced systems.

These policy-induced imbalances and distortions had already set the North Korean economy—the engine ultimately responsible for underwriting state power—on an inauspicious trajectory years ago. By the mid 1980s these cumulative and self-reinforcing difficulties may have helped bring the national economy to the point of stagnation or even negative per capita growth.[28] With the collapse of the Soviet empire, North Korea's economic prospects worsened, as its trade with those countries—heretofore its principal contact with the world economy—contracted suddenly and dramatically.[29] The North Korean economy endured another significant and adverse turn in its international accounts in January 1993, when China, which had become, faute de mieux, its largest trade partner, insisted that the DPRK settle its transactions on a hard-currency basis. These recent jolts and dislocations have left the North Korean economy even less capable of self-sustained development and growth.

What must be apparent to Pyongyang's leadership—in that it is apparent to any outside observers surveying that closed system—is that the North Korean structure possesses no self-correcting mechanisms for redressing long-term economic stagnation or decline. In Leninist doctrine, of course, economic factors are but one component of the overall "correlation of forces" between a socialist state and its imperialist adversaries.[30] Nevertheless, the structural inability to forestall relative or absolute economic decline is a serious matter for any Leninist state insofar as it requires extraordinary countermeasures in noneconomic arenas simply to prevent the correlation of forces with competing states from worsening.

The Regime's Options

How does a regime like the DPRK cope with the prospect of economic decline? How will it attempt to maintain its overall correlation of forces in the international arena while one of the pillars on which this correlation rests is visibly eroding? We may consider some of the alternatives at hand, and their implications for the international community, by weighing three possible adjustments to the material pressures facing the North Korean state: reform, "muddling through," or collapse. Let us consider these separately.

REFORM

From an economic standpoint, "reform"—which is to say the moderation of policy-imposed distortions—would seem to be the most obvious strategy for improving the productivity of the North Korean system and thus ultimately strengthening the sinews of the North Korean state. Since 1984, some observers have divined that North Korea was preparing to embark on a more pragmatic approach to domestic and international economic policy. In this reading, the initial signals of a turn toward a more moderate path were evidenced with the promulgation of the Joint Venture Law (1984) and the advent of the so-called August 3, 1984, campaign to expand consumer goods production by local enterprises.[31] During 1993–1994, students of North Korean affairs have pointed to a number of events that could presage a relaxation, or shift, in official economic policy.[32] Certain port cities will be accorded the status of special economic zones (presumably unencumbered by standard North Korean governance). The Law on Free Economic and Trade Zones has been ratified. The Tumen development project, which as described would involve international financial cooperation with China, Russia, Japan, and even South Korea, absorbing US $30 billion in foreign capital, is being actively promoted. Ongoing negotiations with South Korean *chaebol* (business conglomerates) to secure inter-Korean trade flows, and to entice investment and technology through long-term project commitments from Seoul, are under way. A new foreign direct investment law, a foreign exchange law, and a foreign-invested bank law have been promulgated. Deliberation is occurring over apparently impending legislation on rights to underground mineral and natural resources and on foreign technology imports, and a land lease law for foreigners has been unveiled.

(Some observers also argue that the general suspension in foreign deliveries of the KWP theoretical monthly, *Kulloja,* may indicate a heated debate within the party over the proper direction for economic policy.)

Taken individually or as a whole, these policy decisions and actions describe a tendency whose impact would improve economic performance by restraining the regime's economically destructive habits and behavior. It is one thing, however, to recognize the existence of such tendencies and another to assess their significance.

The fact of such measures should not occasion surprise. In the face of exigence, Marxist-Leninist regimes have always demonstrated considerable tactical flexibility. They have time and again confounded those analysts who predicted them ideologically incapable of embracing the antithetical measures needed for practical purposes or survival. In evaluating North Korea's current reformist tendencies, one must address two questions. First, does the package of emendations thus far enunciated offer the possibility of reversing the downside of the North Korean economy? Second, do these ideological concessions speak to a substantive change of viewpoint in the existing North Korean leadership?

The answer to the first question is the more straightforward. The reformist measures that have been enacted, promulgated, or discussed are patently inadequate to stem North Korea's ongoing economic deterioration, much less jump-start or rejuvenate its flagging economic system. Like the Joint Venture Law that preceded it, North Korea's more recent forays into reformist international policy are halfhearted, neglecting to consider the investors they presumably wish to entice. This neglect is not only apparent in the new legislation. For a 1991 United Nations Development Program conference arranged to promote the Tumen concept, the DPRK sent a delegation of representatives who were, in the words of one Japanese participant, "pitifully unprepared" for those deliberations.[33]

Even if these reformist policies had been competently crafted, however, they would address issues largely peripheral to the current economic malaise. Consider what these proposals and laws do not touch. They avoid the subject of military demobilization and conversion of the war industries. They make no provision for increasing the share of consumption in the national economy. They ignore any amendment of property relations for the rural or urban working populations. They do nothing to strengthen market mechanisms within the domestic economy or to enhance the credibility of the domestic currency. They offer no new avenues for information flows or scientific contacts. They circumvent all questions relating to the government's long-standing default on its international debt obligations. A charitable description of the new initiatives, in relation to the problems at hand, would be "tinkering at the margins."

Moreover, however halfhearted and marginal these efforts may appear, they are countered by policy measures, simultaneously enacted, that press in a completely opposite direction. In April 1992, for example, North Korea promulgated a general wage increase of more than 40 percent for the laboring population. In July 1992 it issued a new currency.[34] These two moves may sound innocuous, but they are not. In the context of chronic goods scarcity, a general wage increase can only throw the consumer market into still greater disequilibrium, further undermining the role of currency-based transactions and reinforcing the primacy of state-determined allocations of supplies in household well-being. By the same token, currency reform, in the context of a command economy, is an occasion to inventory the savings of the populace, to confiscate assets that cannot properly be accounted for, and to garner leads on participants in the unauthorized underground economy. Unlike the new foreign direct investment law (which apparently is still in search of takers), these restrictive measures have already had an impact on the workings of the North Korean economy. It is true that North Korean leaders have recently expressed an interest in the Singapore model.[35] But the notion that policy actions in Pyongyang have brought the DPRK closer to Singapore-style *performance* is a fantasy that reveals just how far removed the current leadership is from the perimeters of genuine reform.

Inferring the intentions of the North Korean leadership in its new regimen of reform is not nearly as conclusive as predicting the consequences. The regime in Pyongyang attempts to keep information about the nation's governance secret, and state strategy is one of the most tightly guarded secrets of all. Under the best of circumstances outsiders seeking to understand the motivations underlying North Korean policy are left to the "study of semi-esoteric communication";[36] more often they are simply forced into semiotic exercises. One may note, however, that the North Korean media have reviewed and analyzed the collapse of the Eastern European states and the downfall of the Soviet Union. They have ascribed these upheavals to precisely the sorts of measures and directions that Western liberals speak of as reforms. As one official assessment put it: "The imperialists . . . have also frantically gone berserk in infiltrating corrupt bourgeois ideology and culture into socialist countries in a bid to inoculate them with the wind of liberalization."[37] Insofar as North Korean officials give all indications of wishing to avoid rather than share in the fates of their erstwhile comrades, one may suspect that Pyongyang is not yet considering a voluntary loosening of control over the economy, society, or information.

It may well be that elements in the North Korean leadership hope to have what they view as the best of both worlds—to maintain tight control over their country and to attract foreign resources at the same time. To date, however, there is little evidence to indicate willingness on the part of the regime to trade any of the former for some of the latter.

MUDDLING THROUGH

One alternative to policy reform is what Lindblom long ago termed *muddling through*—the attempt to cope through improvisations, without reconsidering basic strategy or readjusting fundamental policies.[38] As a description of North Korean government activity since the onset of the revolutions of 1989, muddling through is clearly superior to policy reform. Yet we should also recognize the shortcomings of this paradigm in modeling recent North Korean behavior. The notion of muddling through, as originally expounded, was meant to pertain to the activities of bureaucracies in Western liberal democracies—organizations not rigidly ideological, not locked in self-defined struggles of national survival, and not immobilized when orders fail to flow down from the top. For all these reasons, the vision of muddling through actually presupposes more flexibility with respect to policy change than North Korea has demonstrated on economic questions in recent years. North Korea's present course of action might just as well be termed *barreling through*, for economic policy seems to be informed by a dogged determination to weather the current storm by battening down the hatches and maintaining course.

North Korea's inflexibility in the face of manifest economic decline may in part speak to the outlook and experience of its leadership. The generation of Kim Il Sung has seen much harder times than those it confronts today. Forty-odd years ago, after all, Kim Il Sung was living in an underground bunker beneath a ravaged landscape that was under the shifting control of American and Chinese forces. He emerged from that bunker to build the modern North Korean state. That state is like a diving bell, designed to travel safely through a realm whose pressures would crush weaker constructs.

But even the sturdiest diving bells must eventually surface, and it is not clear how North Korea would locate a breathing space on its present economic course. On the contrary, the present direction in economic policy can only lead to the further debilitation of the national economy and thus ultimately to the debilitation of the KPA as well. On its present direction, then, North Korea can only hope to defend its correlation of forces against the outside world by altering the noneconomic elements in the equation.

In the past, one element that might have seemed amenable to alteration was the political stability of the rival South Korean state. Given what once were the fragile foundations of the South Korean polity, it might have been reasonable to hope that patience would be rewarded by a paralyzing crisis in the ROK or even its collapse. Only fifteen months before President Ronald Reagan took office, for instance, South Korea's strongman was assassinated by his own handpicked security chief. Such an upheaval, however, has become less likely. Since 1987 South Korea has held two open, competitive, and reasonably fair mass presidential elections—the only two of their kind in the entire history of the Korean people. It has also witnessed signal changes in the capabilities of its political parties and important new tendencies for cooperation, coalition building, and consensus seeking on the part of its politically active groups.[39] To bank on the failing political fortunes of the Republic of Korea would thus seem to be an evermore unrealistic bet. If North Korea is to be rescued from its current predicament, it will not be current economic policies that will offer the escape, nor can the DPRK count on what it calls the "incurable malady" of the South Korean system.[40]

COLLAPSE

If policy reform is, for whatever reasons, decisively rejected, and if muddling through cannot redress the state's mounting problems, North Korea faces the prospect of an eventual systemic failure or breakdown—a collapse.

North Korean policy has begun to deal explicitly with this contingency. Official thinking on this score is highlighted by the Ten-Point Program of Great Unity of the Whole Nation for Reunification of the Country, introduced by Kim Il Sung in April 1993. The tenth point in the program deserves special attention. It reads, "Those who have contributed to the great unity of the nation and to the cause of national reunification should be highly estimated."

Should this proposition appear too abstract, a recent DPRK broadcast has helped clarify its meaning. "What is important in appraising people," it explained, "is, above all, to grant special favors to those who have performed feats for the great unity of the nation and the reunification of the country, patriotic martyrs and their descendants."[41] In effect, Pyongyang is now expressly proposing that an insurance policy be issued for the safety and well-being of the North Korean leaders—and, of course, for "their descendants."

Viewed in the context of the DPRK's new ten-point program, North Korea's nuclear program may be seen to have a specific significance. That program was begun many decades earlier, when the current circumstances of the North Korean state were not anticipated. Nuclear weaponry, however, alters the status and increases the options of the states possessing it. It may be seen as an all-purpose instrument of diplomacy, applicable to almost any situation by governments wishing to use it. In its current circumstances, North Korea may view the acquisition of nuclear weapons as the vehicle for extricating it from its current dilemmas.

With nuclear weapons, after all, an unstable North Korea would be a qualitatively greater problem for, and threat to, the international community than it is today. North Korean leaders might correspondingly calculate that the international community would feel more compelled to help prevent instability in the DPRK in the years to come if theirs were a nuclear state. Pyongyang might even hope that the prospect of nuclear instability in the DPRK would prompt the international community to help assure a success-ful transition of leadership from father to son or to offer material assistance to forestall economic breakdown and its attendant uncertainties. Viewed from this perspective, nuclear weaponry may look like a promising instru-ment for helping maintain the existing system.

If North Korea does view nuclear weaponry as a sort of insurance policy for the regime and its leadership, it will be most unlikely to negotiate this opportunity away—no matter what obeisances it may mouth concerning the NPT. At the same time, if the regime views nuclear weaponry as the ultimate guarantor of its domestic stability and international security, it is all the less likely to reform its domestic or international policy. The designs and inten-tions of North Korea's leadership remain well shielded from the outside world. But in attempting to assess North Korea's options and to decipher its strategy, the international community should prepare for the possibility that relations with this most unusual state will become even more tense in the months and years to come than they are today.

Notes

An earlier version of this chapter appeared in *NBR Analysis* 4, no. 3 (September 1993), of the National Bureau of Asian Research.

1. For more information, see "Ministry Asks PRC to Intervene on D.P.R.K.-Czech Issue," *Foreign Broadcast Information Service Daily Report: East Asia* (here-after cited as *FBIS: East Asia*), March 3, 1993, p. 19. For an official North Korean statement, see "Withdrawal of 'Czechoslovak' NNSC Delegation Defended," *FBIS: East Asia,* March 1, 1993, pp. 24–25.

2. For the text of the order, see "Kim Chong-il Orders Army Mobilization," *FBIS: East Asia,* March 8, 1993, pp. 10–11.

3. Lena H. Sun and Jackson Diehl, "N. Korea Reportedly Snubs China," *Wash-ington Post,* April 28, 1993, p. A-13.

4. "Nodong Sinmun: Japan Must 'Act Prudently,'" *FBIS: East Asia,* April 20, 1993, p. 12.

5. Douglas Jehl, "North Korea Isn't Convinced It Should Stay in Nuclear Pact," *New York Times,* June 15, 1993, p. 3. South Korean businessmen were reportedly informed that the ban would be lifted on July 27. See "North Lifts Ban on Foreign Visitors from July 27," *FBIS: East Asia,* July 16, 1993, p. 17.

6. "Russia Said to Restrict Travel to DPRK," *FBIS: East Asia,* July 27, 1993, p. 43.

7. For the full text of the resolution, see " 'News Analysis' Views Resolution," *FBIS: East Asia,* November 2, 1993, pp. 16–17.

8. International Institute of Strategic Studies (IISS), *The Military Balance 1992–93* (London: IISS, 1992), p. 220. By the IISS assessment, KPA active-duty forces totaled 1.132 million in 1991. Larger armies were said to be maintained only by the then USSR (3.988 million), China (3.030 million), the United States (1.918 million), and India (1.265 million)—the four most populous countries in the world at the time.

The U.S. Defense Intelligence Agency (DIA) placed North Korea's total active forces at 1.206 million in a 1991 study. See *North Korea: The Foundations of Military Strength* (Washington, D.C.: DIA, 1991), p. 42. Eberstadt and Banister estimated North Korea's noncivilian male population for 1987 at 1.249–1.323 million. Nicholas Eberstadt and Judith Banister, "Military Buildup in the D.P.R.K.: Some New Indications from North Korean Data," *Asian Survey* 31, no. 11 (November 1991): 1107.

9. Ibid., pp. 1110–11

10. Robert A. Scalapino and Chong-sik Lee, *Communism in Korea* (Berkeley: University of California Press, 1972), p. 919.

11. "ROK: D.P.R.K. Reportedly Develops 1000 Km-Range Missile," *FBIS: East Asia,* August 24, 1992, p. 23.

12. DIA, *North Korea,* p. 60.

13. Central Intelligence Agency, *Korea: The Economic Race between North and South* (Washington, D.C.: National Technical Information Service [NTIS], 1978), p. 3; National Unification Board, *The Economies of South and North Korea* (Seoul: National Unification Board, 1988), p. 30.

14. For a sampling of such pronouncements, see Kim Il Sung, *On the Guidance and Management of the Socialist Economy* (Pyongyang: Foreign Languages Publishing House, 1981).

15. For more details, see Scalapino and Lee, *Communism in Korea,* pp. 969–72.

16. North Korea's approach to land reform, for example, appears to have been more "redemptive" toward landlords than that of other communist countries. See Bruce Cumings, "The Roaring of the Cataract," in *Origins of the Korean War,* vol. 2 (Princeton, N.J.: Princeton University Press, 1990), especially chap. 9.

17. Nicholas Eberstadt and Judith Banister, *The Population of North Korea* (Berkeley, Calif.: Institute of East Asian Studies, 1992), pp. 38–40: estimated ratios of party members to population centers in the year 1987.

18. For further discussion, see Cumings, *Origins of the Korean War,* vol. 2, pp. 298–305.

19. Eberstadt and Banister, *Population of North Korea,* p. 93.

20. Fujio Goto, *Estimates of North Korea's Gross Domestic Product, 1956–59* (Kyoto: Kyoto Sangyo University Press, 1990), p. 68.

21. For the calculations, see Nicholas Eberstadt, *Korea Approaches Reunification,* chap. 1 (forthcoming).

22. Ibid.

23. Personal communications with the author, Pyongyang, May 25, 1990.

24. Wolfgang F. Stolper, *Planning without Facts: Lessons in Resource Allocation from Nigeria's Development* (Cambridge, Mass.: Harvard University Press, 1966).

25. Personal communication with the author, Pyongyang, May 25, 1990.

26. Andrew C. Nahm, *North Korea: Her Past, Reality and Impression* (Kalamazoo: Western Michigan University, Center for Korean Studies, 1978), p. 77.

27. Koo Bon-hak, "Political Economy of Self-Reliance: The Case of North Korea, 1961–1990" (Ph.D. diss., University of Cincinnati, 1992), p. iii.

28. Marina Trigubenko, "Industrial Policy in the D.P.R.K." (Paper presented at the International Symposium on North Korean Economy: Current Situation and Future Prospects, Seoul, September 30–October 1, 1991, cosponsored by Korea Development Institute and Hanguk Kyongje Shinmun).

29. Valentin Moiseyev, "DPRK-U.S.S.R. Trade Patterns" (Paper presented at the International Symposium on the North Korean Economy: Current Situation and Future Prospects, Seoul, September 30–October 1, 1991, cosponsored by Korea Development Institute and Hanguk Kyongje Shinmun).

30. For a "bourgeois" exposition of this concept, see Vernon V. Asparturnian, "Soviet Global Power and the Correlation of Forces," *Problems of Communism* 29 (May–June 1980). For a longer treatment, see Julian Lider, *Correlation of Forces: An Analysis of Marxist-Leninist Concepts* (New York: St. Martin's Press, 1986).

31. See, for example, Kang-suk Rhee, "North Korea's Pragmatism: A Turning Point?" *Asian Survey* 27, no. 8 (August 1987):885–902. See also the following articles by Hy-sang Lee: "North Korea's Economy: The Hidden Opening," *Asian Survey* 28, no. 12 (December 1988):1264–79; "The August 3rd Program of North Korea: A Partial Rollback of Central Planning," *Korea Observer* 21 (Winter 1990): 457–74; "The Economic Reforms of North Korea: The Strategy of Hidden and Assimilable Reforms," *Korea Observer* 23 (Spring 1992):45–78. More recently, see Chris Pritchard, "Hidden Agenda? Despite Nuclear Fracas North Korea Inches toward Capitalism," *Barron's,* December 27, 1993, pp. 13–14.

32. For one such interpretation, see John Merrill, "North Korea: Steering Away from the Shoals," *Asian Survey* 33, no. 1 (January 1993):43–53.

33. Takashi Sugimoto, "The Dawning of Development of the Tumen River Area," International Institute of Global Peace, Policy Paper 75E, March 1992, p. 9.

34. For details, see "Wage Increase Reveals Socialism's 'Superiority,'" *FBIS: East*

Asia, February 25, 1992, p. 18; "Wage Increase Given in April; State Benefits Noted," *FBIS: East Asia,* April 6, 1992, p. 16; "'New Bills' Minted, Circulated Beginning 15 July," *FBIS: East Asia,* July 15, 1992, p. 9.

35. John Merrill, "North Korea in 1993: In the Eye of the Storm," *Asian Survey* 34, no. 1 (January 1994):14.

36. The phrase is borrowed from Morgan Clippinger, "Kim Chong Il in the North Korean Mass Media: A Study of Semi-Esoteric Communication," *Asian Survey* 21, no. 3 (March 1981):289–309.

37. "Nodong Sinmun on Defense of Socialism," *FBIS: East Asia,* July 29, 1992, p. 11.

38. Charles E. Lindblom, "The Science of 'Muddling Through,'" *Public Administration Review* 19 (Spring 1959).

39. For more details, see Nicholas Eberstadt, "Taiwan and South Korea: The 'Democratization' of Outlier States," *World Affairs* 155, no. 2 (Fall 1992):80–89.

40. "D.P.R.K.: South Korean Economy Termed 'Incurable Malady,'" *FBIS: East Asia,* August 25, 1992, p. 12.

41. "Daily Explains Tenth Point in Unity Program," *FBIS: East Asia,* May 13, 1993, p. 21.

2

Korea: Sociopolitical Realities of Reuniting a Divided Nation

Aidan Foster-Carter

Introduction

As a political sociologist, my objective is to focus on the issues and problems that are likely to arise in the eventual, concrete, historical process of reunifying a divided Korea. Conversely, it is not my brief to dwell on a number of key dimensions or preliminaries of this process, including the economic and financial dimensions or the international context.

Korea's reunification will be expensive, like Germany's and for the same reasons. Both transitional subsidies and pensions to individuals and firms, on the one hand, and new investment in modernizing North Korea's decrepit economy, on the other, will be multibillion-dollar enterprises stretching over at least a decade. The sheer magnitude of the task will necessitate direct foreign investment on a massive scale, notwithstanding any nationalist instincts to the contrary. This expense, although shared between the Korean government and both Korean and foreign private business, is bound to affect and color the social and especially political dimensions of the unification process. (I will amplify this later in the chapter.)

Similarly, the international context will also be influential. Actual outcomes in any situation are always the product of interaction among economic, political, and social factors and processes and between national and international dimensions. So here again, the fact that this chapter focuses on matters internal to Korea by no means implies that external factors are unimportant. Recalling the way Korea got divided in the first place, casually and arbitrarily, reminds us that outside forces can sometimes be utterly decisive.

Another and no less important methodological lesson of 1945 is the Weberian one warning against excessively structural explanations and insisting on the role of sheer contingency and the inherently unpredictable in determining the course of events. Here, just as the era of globalization means that international influences are ineluctable (there will be no hermit kingdoms in the twenty-first century), so the end of the cold war cannot but add to this already inbuilt factor of predictability. To be concrete: although we do not know how China will be after Deng Xiaoping or whether Boris Yeltsin will survive or even whether China and Russia will survive or break up, what is certain is that how history eventually answers these questions will form a crucial backdrop to the process of reunification in Korea.

Nonetheless, it should also be stated that Korea in the 1990s is in a far stronger position to influence its own fate than it was in the 1940s—let alone the 1890s. To that extent, I hope that bracketing the international context may not be altogether inappropriate.

Reunification will come about in one of two broad ways. It may be gradual, that is to say, an evolutionary process of increasing reconciliation, contacts, cooperation, and ultimate integration between the two existing states and regimes on the peninsula. Or it will be sudden, by which a revolutionary process occasioned by the collapse of North Korea will lead to a process of absorption comparable to the German case.

The "collapsist" scenario seems the most plausible. Although I fully share the hope, which is widespread in South Korea, for a gradual, stable, peaceful, and inexpensive evolution, indications point to collapse. The key element of my reasoning is that North Korea cannot continue indefinitely as it is. Economic contraction at around 5 percent annually must eventually precipitate implosion and collapse of the economy, meaning an inability to function even at the most basic level (i.e., supply food and other elementary needs). This in turn will trigger political protest and action, in either or both of two forms—an interelite coup, probably military, or grassroots protests. Either way, the North Korean regime will be overthrown. As in Germany, there will then be a strong popular demand for immediate integration. This will be irresistible. A workable legitimation or the continued existence of a non–Kim Il Sungist North Korean state in the 1990s cannot possibly be constructed.

Although in principle a "collapse" could be avoided by embracing economic reforms in the manner of China and Vietnam, this would not imply an alternative to the end of the Kim Il Sung government. This is because perestroika inexorably breeds glasnost. Increased awareness of Southern prosperity could not fail to undermine Kim Il Sung's carefully constructed quarantine and with it the legitimacy of his regime. Because the great leader is no fool, this doubtless explains North Korea's resolute and explicit refusal of the reform path—to the exasperation of the Chinese leadership, among others.

Even if Kim Il Sungism were somehow to prove more durable than the above arguments suggest, the death of Kim Il Sung will provide a window and a trigger for the end of the North Korean regime and reunification with the South at some point within the next decade. The above arguments are reinforced by, although independent of, the North Korean government's current apparent willingness to provoke a serious crisis by its noncompliance with the Non-Proliferation Treaty.

At all events, given these views, this chapter assumes that reunification in practice will have been occasioned by the collapse of North Korea. Managing it will thus be viewed as essentially a task that will confront South Korea. Some version of the German scenario seems likely. Otherwise, one is left with the alleged alternative whereby old enemies become not just friends but lovers, leopards change their spots, and Seoul and Pyongyang walk hand in hand into a new dawn. Such wishful thinking ignores the key issues of power and legitimation in the whole process. Meanwhile, most of the factors to be examined here will, I hope, also be pertinent, mutatis mutandis, even in a gradualist scenario.

Some Methodological Comments

Underlying the above are some implicit arguments about method. Like anyone working on North Korea, I have spent much time reflecting on not only what we know but how we know we know it and on how to choose between Weber's "plausible stories" in the many areas where we cannot yet attain certain knowledge. There is more and better empirical evidence than is sometimes realized, ranging from Eberstadt's pioneering work on population and labor force data to the neglected source on widespread and persistent system malfunctioning that is provided by the collected works of none other than Kim Il Sung himself.[1] Where such evidence is lacking, we can and must employ deductive methods: rigorously thinking through the sociologic of the situation.

An important aid is offered by comparative insights. North Korea is not sui generis. In its origins and functioning, it clearly belongs to a distinct—if now also all but extinct—species of regimes that may be called state socialist, communist, or Stalinist, according to taste. Although eschewing any mechanical reading off and making due allowance for particularity, there are lessons to be learned, analogies to be pursued, and comparisons to be drawn.

I thus come down firmly on the nomothetic side of the Methodenstreit. Although no positivist—following Habermas, I believe that social science must also embrace hermeneutics and critique—I see the task of the social sciences as centrally including the search for general propositions. I freely confess that the challenge of trying to account for North Korea has sharpened this conviction. As against the shrill and ludicrous claims of *juche* (sovereignty) to uniqueness and the omnipotence of voluntarism, in my writings I have tried to show that, on the contrary, Kim Il Sung can no more escape sociology than he can mortality. North Korea is certainly an extreme case, but it is not an exception; it is rather an epigone, and it will not ultimately avoid the fate of others of its ilk.

Having thus sketched my general methodological stance, let me add one or two remarks particular to this chapter. Some of the above points will be more implicit than explicit, partly because, although a comparativist by conviction, I am not so in expertise and partly because it is difficult to footnote the future. In what follows, then, I shall endeavor to exercise a creative but also rigorous sociological imagination.

Kim's Children

Having just made the case for nomothetic social science, let me now shift to hermeneutic mode. The place to begin, I think, is with the thoughts and feelings of North Koreans now or a few years hence. Despite the claims to *yuilsasang* (monolithic ideology), and indeed the efforts to impose it, they will be in at least some respects diverse. For instance, consider an age and generation.

Thanks to Eberstadt's pathbreaking work, one thing we know for sure is how many North Koreans remember their past.[2] Those over sixty as of mid 1990, and thus with at least a semiadult awareness of living in a different kind of society (aged fifteen or over in 1945), numbered some 1.25 million. Even in 1990, those pensioners were far outnumbered by their more than twenty million compatriots who were younger. Of course, the relative gap is widening with every passing year.

Adding the next decile below (those aged fifty to fifty-nine in mid 1990) gives a further 1.4 million. This group remembers something of Japanese rule and are also likely to retain vivid personal memories of kin from whom they subsequently became separated.

Coming at it from the other end, those aged one to thirty-four in 1990, and hence unable to remember the Korean War or immediate reconstruction even as infants, totaled some 15.4 million, or almost three-quarters of the population. Once again, in subsequent years both the absolute and relative gaps will widen and go on widening.

At most, only one North Korean in five is old enough to remember either another society or lost relatives. Nothing follows unambiguously from this, especially on the macrolevel. Although we may assume that those with lost relatives grieve, and thus have a personal motive for reunification or at least getting back in touch, we cannot be sure how many of the old still thank the great leader for their deliverance or curse him for a life in some ways more onerous and intrusive than under the Japanese.

Of course, those older will have told their children how they lived. Such domestic socialization will in some spheres challenge the relentless efforts by the state to monopolize citizens' hearts and minds. In particular, it is inconceivable that Christians and other religious believers will not have endeavored quietly to pass on their faiths.

One could pursue such speculations further. For instance, I do not mean to imply that growing up under Kim Il Sungism has been a homogeneous experience over the four postwar decades. On the contrary, there may well have been at least three watersheds. Socially, as shown once again by Eberstadt, there is a huge and curious disjunction around 1970. Whereas the 1950s and 1960s saw massive geographic and occupational mobility, thereafter those processes slowed almost to a standstill. Thus urban dwellers rose from 17.7 percent in 1953 to 54.2 percent in 1970; yet by 1987, the figure was only 59.6 percent. In the 1980s only one household in twenty on average relocated each year, as compared to four times as many in South Korea.

North Koreans born after 1970, then, who have experienced much less if any mobility than those older, already numbered some 8.8 million by 1990; by now they will be some 11.3 million, or half the population. This social watershed circa 1990 approximately coincides and doubtless correlates with a political watershed. Although the gradual tightening of the totalitarian apparatus of social control was a continuous process from the beginning, the late 1960s seem to have marked a particular turning point. As well as the capture of the *Pueblo* and the raid on the Blue House, this was an era of major purges and an era when North Koreans married to foreigners were forced either to divorce them or to flee abroad. The space for any kind of autonomous civil society, already small, thereafter dwindled to almost nothing.

The third watershed, which is both more recent and more gradual, relates to economic growth. The slowdown of the economy in the 1980s, and its reversal in the 1990s, must affect different generations' life experiences. Once again the half of the population born after 1970 will have had proportionately less experience of a steadily improving standard of living and rather more of stagnation and ultimate decline. Although aggregate gross national product may not have started shrinking until 1989, there is evidence of a squeeze on living standards in the early 1980s.

Observations such as these can be no more than raw materials for attitudinal or behavioral predictions. They may nonetheless be a useful first step to estimating possible differences of outlook from known differences of experience.

Social Stratification—Estates

Another social division in North Korea, this time man-made rather than biologic, is likely to be a better predictor of attitudes. Although not officially confirmed, it is widely accepted that the North Korean regime classifies all its citizens into both broad categories and more-detailed subdivisions on the basis of either ascribed or achieved degrees of loyalty.[3] Ascription is paramount inasmuch as these categories are the ultimate determinant of opportunities and privileges such as where you live (countryside, town, or Pyongyang), your job, whether your children may go to university, and even how much food you eat. It thus seems appropriate to call these groups *estates* (Weber's *Standen*) rather than social classes.

The consequences of such a system seem clear, given that the loyal estate constitutes at most one-quarter of the population, with the core elite numbering around 200,000, or a bare 1 percent. By contrast, fully 50 percent of the population is classified as wavering, and a further 20 percent, as actively hostile. These last two categories, totaling between two-thirds and three-quarters of the North Korean citizenry, experience both privation and active and arbitrary discrimination throughout their lives. If they were not hostile at the outset, it strains credulity to believe that they will not have become so over time. The concept of *han*, not exactly unknown in South Korea as a response to unjust suffering and inequality, must be working overtime north of the demilitarized zone (DMZ). This is curiously overlooked by those who give high ratings to the grip that Kim Il Sung's regime has in the 1990s on his subjects' hearts and minds.

What can we say about the attitudinal and behavioral dispositions that North Koreans will bring to reunification? Several speculations are offered:

General social mores are likely to be conservative, given both the continuity from the Japanese era and the official morality of Stalinism. North Koreans have had no exposure to the varied and overlapping pressures of Western culture, individualism, liberalism, or a consumer society. After half a century apart from a South Korea that conversely has been much influenced and transformed (though neither overwhelmed nor destroyed) by those pressures, theirs will be a very different mind-set from that south of the DMZ.

Yet to say this immediately raises further questions, which moreover have the merit of treating North Koreans as something more than automata or passive recipients of their rulers' plans. Almost certainly, North Korea is a profoundly hypocritical society. Even in less extreme variants of Stalinism, the phenomenon was widely documented of citizens' active or passive withdrawal. Although prudently conforming to outward norms and forms, ordinary people resent their exploitation and are well aware of the sordid bribery and influence peddling, which is how things get done in reality, as opposed to the official rhetoric, which fools nobody.

The consequence of this is likely to be a certain skepticism, cynicism, even nihilism. Politically, as has happened elsewhere, a root and branch hostility toward socialism could develop, in reaction to decades of that verbal and ideological currency's devaluation under Kim Il Sung. In that sense, North Koreans will be politically as well as socially conservative.

There is one disposition that North Koreans assuredly share with all those who have lived under similar regimes. For almost half a century, the link between personal effort and reward has been severed. As in all other former communist countries, acquiring the capitalist work ethic will be a shock. Comparative evidence suggests, however, that this is only a transitional problem. Before long, the preferability of a wage and an outcome determined by one's own efforts rather than arbitrary fiat outweighs the initial jolt.

One intriguing question is what will fill the huge ideological void that will be left when the edifice of Kim Il Sungism collapses? Because few, if any, North Koreans are still true believers, this will not be a major psychological trauma. On the contrary, many who have long resented the abolition of their privacy may not even wish to replace Kimism but would rather rejoice in the homely values of family and breathing freely.

What seems likely, nonetheless, is that as elsewhere the gap will be filled by a tendency to atavism and reaction. That is, there will be a quest for and an embrace of creeds and symbols that either preceded or opposed communism, similar to the recovery of Saint Petersburg in post-Soviet Russia. In North Korea, as in other countries, this will certainly mean an explosion of religious belief, welcomed and encouraged, of course, by coreligionists from the South. Church spires will sprout in the new Pyongyang as they once did in the old.

Overview and Prediction

In this section, I discuss the likely experiences and attitudes that North Koreans will bring to reunification. Overall, the picture seems to me a more promising one than in the corresponding German situation. Unlike East Germans, most North Koreans have nothing to lose but their chains. Citizens of the former German Democratic Republic enjoyed the highest standard of living in the communist bloc. Life had its controls, but it also had its compensations.

By contrast, after almost half a century, the regime started by Kim Il Sung is still offering his subjects the same old blood and toil, sweat and tears. Things are getting worse, not better. That East Germans, unlike North Koreans, knew what they were missing because they could watch the other side's television, although true, seems beside the point. However ignorant North Koreans may be of living standards south of the DMZ, though they probably know more than they are often given credit for, what counts is that their own lives are a hellish grind—and getting worse.

Their patience will snap eventually. But, in sharp and crucial contrast to East Germany and indeed all of the former communist Eastern Europe, for post-Kim North Korea the only way is up; things are already at rock bottom. In what will certainly be a difficult and demanding transition, Seoul can at least take comfort from this. Even if several million North Koreans spend a year or more living on rations from the South's rice stockpile, they will be much better off. Similarly, if several million more spend a year or two getting paid very little for doing very little, that too may not be so different or so awful compared with what they have become used to. In Germany the first emotional flush of reunification dissipated fairly rapidly into what is becoming a long hard slog of tough reconstruction and mutual mistrust. Without making light of the difficult policy dilemmas that Seoul will face and that are discussed in the next section, it does seem appropriate to mention this key difference.

Reunification: Policy Issues and Dilemmas

In this section, I analyze some of the key specific areas and issues for reunification policy. All the earlier cautions apply, and again the predominance of politics, policy, and contingency must be stressed.

Reunification is something that will need to be managed; it will not just happen. And like anything that people do, it can be done well or badly.

Equally, policy making is rendered difficult by the role of sheer contingency. No policy maker can predict the future, and even skilled navigators (and they don't come better than in Seoul) can be blown off course or even sunk by unforeseen storms. Foremost among these risks are political ones. In what follows, a mariner's chart is delineated.

Just as South Korea's "late development" meant it could learn and borrow from those who had gone before, Germany's—and Yemen's—experience should be of enormous value, at least in spotlighting what not to do. No currency exchange rate should be established that will at a stroke render all industry in the former North Korea noncompetitive.

If South Korea's remarkable development owes more to skilled government-business coordination than to the workings of a putatively free market, then it follows that many of the skills and policy instruments appropriate for reunification are already in place. Although it is true that Korea, Inc., has been declining and, ceteris paribus, would continue to decline as economic liberalization gradually gained ground, nonetheless the instincts are still available and can readily be revived. Chances are, when the time comes, it will still be possible in the mid 1990s for Kim Young-sam to instruct, say, Pohang to take over and modernize the Kim Chack steelworks, and lo it shall be done. Even though the *chaebol* have become much more autonomous of government, it is reckoned that a combination of their own rivalries plus the likely mood come reunification will ensure that they scramble, dutifully and competitively, to rebuild North Korea as they are bid.

This was not an option in Germany's more-mild social capitalism. And although the challenge of reunification will be South Korea's biggest yet, Seoul's past success in turning around deeply unpromising circumstances against seemingly overwhelming odds is surely not immaterial. In business terms, the confidence factor seems positive, and the management team is the best there is.

If Korea, Inc., refers to Seoul's policy skills (culturally mediated, no doubt) in successfully yoking state and capital for national unification, the question is raised whether South Korea still retains a spirit of cultural collectivism for the supreme national task of reunification. Granted, the signals are mixed. Some opinion polls suggest that reunification is either not seen as an especially high priority in practice or is seen as a source of worry. Both positive and negative auguries are examined in the sections that follow, such as the impact of religion and families and the question of whether it will be desirable or even possible to maintain some kind of controls at the DMZ. Overall, however, Korea has available a stock of cultural cement, which Germany did not.

These are potential forces in Korea that have no German equivalent, given the much greater mobility before the Berlin Wall was torn down. It should not be difficult for policy makers to harness their likely energies and desires. In the event that it is deemed desirable and proves possible to maintain some form of influx control at the DMZ, then joining separated families should be a priority. Even making initial contacts will be a massive bureaucratic, computer, and logistic exercise, as amply shown by the much smaller yet still huge exercise conducted on Seoul TV a few years ago. When Southern families are joined by Northern family members, the Southerners should take the financial responsibility for them. The public treasury will have enough commitments; it will need to spread the burdens. The numbers of North Koreans thus admitted should help to ease the South's tight labor market, without overwhelming it. However, additional workers can be recruited where demand and supply match. Mining is one obvious candidate.

Much more desirable, however, would be to encourage separated families to go back to North Korea rather than vice versa. Older generations may in any case yearn to return to their ancestral homes and burial grounds. Younger generations may need, and should be given, attractive financial incentives not just to relocate but to invest and start businesses in the North. Such a policy raises the question of property claims and whether or how far to entertain them. The spectacle of former *yangban* (elites) returning to reclaim their estates might not go down too well and would in any case be inconsistent with this class's dispossession in South Korea. A balance must be struck between the claims of returnees and locals because reconstruction will require commitment from both groups. In practice this may not prove too difficult. Any and all investment will be welcomed in North Korea, not only for returning exiles but for other Koreans and, for that matter, foreigners. The tasks will be huge.

The Churches

Religious organizations—especially Christian but also Buddhist, Chondogyo, and others, certainly not forgetting the Unification Church—can and doubtless will play an important role. Whereas governments direct and businesses invest—both processes that have an initial potential for conflict and pain—the churches are in a position to represent civil society rather than authority or profit. Hence churches can mediate, heal, and generally smooth the path. As well as reestablishing old links, proselytizing, and doing social welfare work, the churches can fulfill a vital function by providing a relatively neutral context in which North and South Koreans can meet on more or less equal terms to begin to get to know one another again after half a century of separation.

Should the DMZ Be Kept?

I now want to discuss the issue that I have mentioned only in passing. If and when North Korea collapses, the DMZ will still be there. Hence immediate free movement between North and South will not be feasible. There will be barriers, mines, and troops still in place. Many in South Korea, perhaps shamefacedly, will be glad of this. Government and citizenry alike may fear the impact of a sudden uncontrolled influx of Northerners in search of a promised land that by definition would elude them in such numbers and on that basis, namely, as refugees or mendicants.

South Korea would much rather that unification take an evolutionary course. As already mentioned, this would enable a much more controlled process, preferable on economic, political, and social grounds, as opposed to an inherently unpredictable and uncontrollable "big bang," in which the barriers simply fall and formal unification is virtually instantaneous, as occurred in Germany. This, however, is where we enter the unpredictable political realm. It is likely that a Northern collapse—or an earlier phase of civil unrest, which in some ways would pose a trickier dilemma—could lead to a flood of refugees trying to cross the DMZ. No doubt South Korean leaders would appeal to them to return home and be patient. They might obey, or they might not, in which case, would guns be pointed at them? would they be fired? There are also ways around the DMZ, by boat, for instance.

Hence it seems to me that the actual circumstances of reunification, as well as the preliminaries, will be such that the gradualist option is simply not feasible. It may not be possible to hold the line. In this case, the border may have to be opened; for the rest, policy will have to proceed in a context of laissez-faire, especially as regards mobility.

It is a moot point whether big bang or gradualism would do more to break down or more to sustain the psychological and perceptual barriers that are bound to persist between North and South Koreans. As with *Wessis* and *Ossis* in Germany, only more so, no magic wand or gush of goodwill will erase the cultural differences that have arisen from half a century of not just division but divergence. The two will talk differently, dress differently, look differently (owing to poor diet, Northerners will be smaller and thinner), and think differently.

It is easy to envisage a situation arising, as it did in Germany, where the dream turns sour and mutual animosities begin to breed. South Koreans, like West Germans, could resent picking up the tab for their backward siblings. North Koreans, unlike East Germans, will not get poorer, and yet like them they may come to resent what they perceive as the slowness of improvement and the snobbery and selfishness of their richer cousins.

It could go either way. The big bang, if it happens, could ease integration. Young North Koreans in particular—and they are the majority—may turn into South Koreans with enthusiasm and surprising ease, just as many young South Korean immigrants have turned, more or less, into Americans in the past three decades. People can and do adapt culturally. Politically, however, the fear is that big bang would stoke prejudice in the South, based on fears of being swamped.

Alternatively, the evolutionary path, despite its apparent smoothness, runs the risk of entrenching and perpetuating distinct Northern and Southern identities—particularly if, as we discuss next, it is decided to continue administering Northern Korea from Pyongyang.

Administrative Structures

As in Germany, the question will arise as to how to administer North Korea. Whatever happens, it will doubtless not be done by the nominal office that still exists in Seoul for the purpose. To be decided will be whether to keep the new provinces of Chagang and Ryanggang, created in the far North, or to merge them back into Pyongan and Hamgyong. More fundamental is the question of whether to administer North Korea separately and, if so, how. Retaining the DMZ would settle the matter one way. The converse is not necessarily true; even the big bang could be consistent with, and might be mitigated by, a decision to continue government from (or at least via) Pyongyang.

This will be a difficult decision. On the one hand, keeping Pyongyang in business as a quasi capital would at least give that city a function and thousands of its inhabitants a job. On the other hand, Korean instincts and practices in both ancient and modern history have opted for centralized rule from Seoul. Besides, former officials under Kim Il Sung might lack either the skills or the legitimacy (or both) to manage the transition back to capitalism. Or they might be good at it, so much so as to constitute a political force in their own right.

As the above example shows, the decision about administration is also and ultimately political in its implications. This raises the fascinating, if as yet unanswerable, question of how unification will affect the domestic politics of Korea as a whole. Here the German outcome seems unlikely, given the fissiparous state and nonideological basis of South Korea's existing political parties. Ambitious North Koreans may join the Democratic Liberal

Party (DLP), although the Center for Korean Women and Politics (CKWP) might emulate some of its East European counterparts and belatedly discover the virtues of social democracy.

Alternatively, given the regional cast of existing South Korean political alignments, some form of Northern party might emerge. In view of the North's one to two population ratio gap with the South, any such formation would need to build alliances. Theoretically, a DLP-Northern coalition might outpoll the DLP. Because after unification the North is likely to be competing with, and to be favored over, Cholla for new investment, however, such an alliance must be reckoned unlikely.

Employment and Unemployment

The work question has sociopolitical as well as economic dimensions. On the one hand, as in all former communist economies, rationalization will entail a massive shakeout of labor. On the other hand, the social costs of this process need to be minimized. As ever, there are several aspects.

Even more than in transitions elsewhere, the burden of labor shedding in North Korea is likely to fall heavily on women because they constitute a clear majority of the formal labor force: 7.15 million in 1987, as against 5.367 million men.[4] That makes 57 percent of the total. Even if one adds, in Eberstadt's estimate, the unreported extra 1.25 million males in the armed forces (which are active in the construction sector, in addition to their military duties), females are still in the majority. In the likely atmosphere of a postcommunist and still Confucian society where job losses need to be found, it seems that this particular revolutionary gain will be rolled back. This may even be experienced as a gain by some of those women concerned because the "double day" of formal plus domestic labor (plus study sessions and the like) means that at present their burden is especially onerous. Similarly, North Korea's vaunted universal creche system may well be threatened; again, in this particular context some mothers may be glad to see more of their children. But the choice is unlikely to be theirs.

What to do with the massive North Korean army will be a particular dilemma. Although the great majority are conscripts, and although service conditions are reportedly bad and unpopular, unleashing hordes of young men to swell the ranks of the unemployed would be risky. There may be a partial alternative. South Korea too has an overlarge conscript army. It also has a labor shortage, and there have been suggestions that it is time to move to a professional force. Although it would no doubt involve a degree of retraining (there will be a lot of that in every field in the new North Korea), it might be an idea to push soldiering in the ranks as a preferential career option for Northerners, at least in the first instance. The existing Southern officer corps would not be displaced, although it will need to open itself to talent from the former Korean People's Army.

In principle, it should be possible to use the skills of North Korea's existing doctors, teachers, engineers, and other professionals. Many, probably most, will require their skills upgraded. Integrating the organizational systems of North and South will not be easy, which may be another argument for gradualism and a continued quasi DMZ.

Of these two aspects—skills and systems—it seems likely that the North Korean education system has produced near-universal literacy, like its Southern counterpart. Despite a predominance of science and technology at the college level, however, it is doubtful whether overall specialist knowledge is at world level except in a few fields, of which armaments could be one. As for systems, in some fields, notably health and social security, North Korea claims to operate a free and comprehensive service, as opposed to South Korea's partial and insurance-based system. Quality is likely to be highly uneven, however—or, more exactly, stratified according to rank—so the perhaps inevitable loss of these provisions may not diminish actual welfare. Alternatively, a bold government might contemplate extending the claimed gains of the North's welfare state to the country as a whole.

Winners and Losers: Sectors and Regions

The social impact of reunification will be uneven in terms of both economic sectors and geographic regions in North Korea. At least some winners and losers, however, can be predicted with some confidence.

Economic sectors likely to feel the pinch include agriculture and the chemical industry. What to do with the North Korean farm sector will be a dilemma, but it will probably be decollectivized into small private holdings of the kind that are usual in the South. But much Northern agriculture is on marginal land. In a unified Korea, the South will be the rice bowl. The quest for yields will exacerbate the problems of chemical overuse and soil exhaustion. Although the western plains of Pyongan and Hwangbae will stay in business, marginal upland areas may become depopulated, unless they shift to ranching. But then again, subsidizing small farmers for political reasons is not unknown in South Korea; it may prove possible to extend the principle.

Although all industry will shed labor as it acquires long-overdue new equipment and much-needed capital intensiveness, chemicals look to be especially noncompetitive—not least as a consequence of the great leader's obsessions, such as the artificial fabric vinalon, which will doubtless die with him.

The omens elsewhere are more propitious, assuming new investment and despite substantial labor shedding. Most mining may remain viable, especially in precious and nonferrous metals and iron. Coal may be scaled down. Light industry for export has good prospects, provided wages can be kept competitive. The potential for tourism is enormous, especially around Kumgang-san and Paekdo-san, which will attract millions of long-excluded Southern visitors.

Conducting a similar exercise on a regional basis suggests that favored regions will comprise two related categories — growth corridors and border areas. The existing Pusan-Seoul corridor will split into a V as it extends northwest to Pyongyang and on to China on one side (the main line, no doubt) and northeast to Wonsan and on to Russia on the other side (the branch line, perhaps). Anyone along these major arteries-to-be, especially the Pusan-Seoul corridor, should be in business. Other places may not fare as well. As for border areas, Sinuiju and the prematurely hyped Tumen border zone should both benefit; at the other end, now is the time to start buying land and property in and around Kaesong, against the day when it becomes within commuting and business range of Seoul.

As mentioned earlier, finding a new role for Pyongyang will not be straightforward. With so many resources having been poured into it (albeit often into grand creations of zero economic value), and containing as it does some 10 percent of the North's population, this potential garden city cries out for an imaginative and appropriate use. Although its existing light industrial base can be augmented, additional functions will be required, such as a university city for either new seats of learning or some old ones "encouraged" to move out of Seoul. The bold stroke, however, would be the Brasilia option: to make Pyongyang the seat of government or at least move some ministries there. That would do much to advance integration.

A Final Miscellany

Many aspects of the multifaceted process of reunification have yet to be considered, such as the country's name and flag. In an absorption scenario, one supposes it will be *Taehan minguk* and the *taegukki*. More generous would be those agreed on for the two (so far) pan-Korean sports teams: Korea and an outline of the peninsula. The name *Choson* will probably be a lost cause.

One process that will advance reunification where it counts, in people's hearts, is intermarriage. There will be a pattern to this. The only North

Korean joke I have ever heard (and which incidentally confirms that virilocality remains the norm there) is a maiden's plea: never mind if he's old and ugly, as long as he's from Pyongyang. Similarly, matrimony may yet prove to be an avenue of social mobility southward and upward. A twist to this, two decades hence, is that the South's future deficit of young women, caused by the current misuse of amniocentesis for gender-specific abortions, may well lead to more Southern men seeking Northern brides—and hence pushing their Northern peers into involuntary bachelorhood.

What, finally, of revenge? Not the least of gradualism's problems, morally and politically, is that it ignores the matter of the Northern gulag: at least 100,000 strong and in predictably barbaric conditions (as the 1992 escapees testified). When the survivors at last come stumbling out, the demand for revenge and atonement will be acute.

The question of how far to prosecute yesterday's direct and indirect murderers or torturers is a difficult one, not just in former communist states but in a wide range of postdictatorial societies. Because this category includes South Korea, it might seem inconsistent or impolitic to arraign senior North Korean figures, assuming any remain, while not bringing Chun Doo Hwan to book for Kwangju. Probably smaller fry will pay for their crimes, if anybody does. The introduction of a judicial system and the rule of law in North Korea may in any case enable citizens to bring their own private prosecutions.

But at the government level, it may be necessary for the victim to see the butcher go free in order to build a new future unblighted by the rekindling of old conflicts that would follow if every crime were truly avenged. This will be a difficult pill to swallow in a political culture where hurts ancient and modern are keenly felt and assiduously kept alive. There does not seem to be a *sokdam* (folk saying) that translates as "forgive and forget." Reunification will require one.

Conclusion

This chapter attempts to raise a wide range of sociopolitical issues that are likely to arise in the process of Korea's eventual reunification. The more we think ahead, creatively as well as rigorously, the better the chance that Korea's longed-for reunification will be more the dream it should be than the nightmare it might be.

Notes

1. Aidan Foster-Carter, "North Korea in Pacific Asia," in Chris Dixon and David Drakakis-Smith, eds., *Economic and Social Development in Pacific Asia* (London: Routledge, 1993).
2. Nicholas Eberstadt, "Population and Labor Force in North Korea: Trends and Implications" (Paper presented at a conference at the Korean Development Institute, Seoul, September 1991).
3. Richard Kagan, Richard Matthew Oh, and David Weissbrodt, *Human Rights in the Democratic People's Republic of Korea* (Washington, D.C.: Asia Watch, 1988), p. 34.
4. Eberstadt, "Population and Labor Force," table 7.

Selected Bibliography

Australian National Korean Studies Centre. *Korea to the Year 2000: Implications for Australia.* Canberra: Commonwealth of Australia, 1992.

Eberstadt, Nicholas. "Population and Labor Force in North Korea: Trends and Implications." Paper presented at a conference at the Korean Development Institute, Seoul, September 1991. I have not yet seen his monograph *The Population of North Korea* (coauthored with Judith Banister) Berkeley, Calif.: Institute of East Asian Studies.

Foster-Carter, Aidan. "The Gradualist Pipedream: Prospects and Pathway to Korean Reunification." Paper written for a conference in Canberra, Commonwealth of Australia, March 1992.

———. *Korea's Coming Reunification: Another East Asian Superpower?* London: Economist Intelligence Unit, 1992.

———. "North Korea in Pacific Asia." In Chris Dixon and David Drakakis-Smith, eds., *Economic and Social Development in Pacific Asia.* London: Routledge, 1993.

Kagan, Richard, Richard Matthew Oh, and David Weissbrodt. *Human Rights in the Democratic People's Republic of Korea.* Washington, D.C.: Asia Watch, 1988.

Kornai, Janos. *The Socialist System: The Political Economy of Communism.* Oxford, Eng., and Princeton, N.J.: Princeton University Press, 1992.

McCormack, Gavan. "Kim Country: Hard Times in North Korea." *New Left Review,* no. 198 (March/April 1993).

3

German Lessons for Managing the Economic Cost of Korean Reunification

Jongryn Mo

Introduction

The reunification of Korea was a dream of most Koreans even before the reunification of Germany in 1990. South Koreans reacted to the events in Germany with envy and a renewed hope for their own reunification. As the costs of German reunification mounted, however, Koreans began to worry.

South Korea now favors a multistage reunification process in which economic and political union will be gradually achieved through negotiations between North and South Korea. South Korea envisions a negotiated merger instead of the one-sided absorption that characterized the German union.

South Korea, however, cannot overlook the possibility of a one-sided takeover of North Korea. Whether Korean reunification takes the form of a negotiated or a sudden merger depends not only on South Korean policy but also on the future of the North Korean regime. If North Korea collapses, South Korea will have no choice but to absorb North Korea so as to avoid the specter of anarchy in North Korea. If North Korea implements a far-reaching reform program, North and South Korea may be able to negotiate a gradual merger. But most observers seem to doubt the capacity of the North Korean regime for reform.

Given the strong possibility of a one-sided merger in Korea, South Korea must take lessons from the German experience. Above all, the view that a German-type absorption is inevitably costly must be reevaluated. South Korea needs to plan how to manage and control a one-sided merger and thus avoid some of the costly mistakes that West Germany made.

Some of the factors responsible for the high cost of reunification in Germany were clearly beyond the control of German policy makers.[1] The collapse of East Germany's traditional export markets devastated the East German economy; other problems resulting from ignorance could also have been avoided. Reunifying different national economies had never been done before, and Korean policy makers can learn from the mistakes made in Germany.

Germany's leaders selected policies—such as the speed and timing of economic union, the hands-off wage policy in East Germany after union, and the decision to restore property rights to former owners of East German properties—despite warnings about their adverse consequences. It is difficult to predict whether Korea will be able to avoid the same mistakes without knowing the domestic political context of German policy. How German policy makers reacted to reunification issues was shaped by the domestic political conflict over them. If Korean domestic political conditions at the time of reunification are similar to those of Germany in 1990, Korean policy makers, like their German counterparts, will have similar incentives to choose the same policies.

My argument is that the domestic political situation in Korea will be sufficiently different from that of Germany at the time of reunification to enable Korean policy makers to avoid most of the problems that have plagued German reunification.

German Lessons for Preparing and Consolidating Reunification

Managing the economics of reunification requires different policy responses at different stages of reunification. The German experience provides lessons in economic management over the entire course of reunification (i.e., before, during, and after the formal act of reunification). Because the rest of the chapter focuses on economic management at the time of reunification (i.e., the terms of reunification that West Germany chose in 1990), this section touches on two other stages of the German lesson.

South Korea's prereunification economic policy centers around expand-

ing economic cooperation with North Korea, which will entail certain political consequences that South Korea must incorporate in evaluating its
policy objectives. The German experience with intra-German trade before
reunification can help Korean policy makers identify the likely political
consequences of intra-Korea economic cooperation.

The political consequences of trade have long been a controversial issue
in the academic debate. Liberal economists maintain that trade promotes
peace through economic interdependence. Realists counter that trade between two countries can result in an asymmetric dependence that can be
used as an instrument of national power by the less dependent country.[2] The
liberal view, however, seems to dominate the policy debate in South Korea.[3]
Those who hold the liberal view also claim that the German experience
supports their position.

The lessons of intra-German economic cooperation, however, are complex and show that many of the benefits that economic cooperation is
supposed to bring do not exist. First, economic cooperation before reunification did not reduce the cost of reunification.[4] East German trade with
West Germany before reunification was not guided by market principles,
and there is no compelling evidence that North Korea will be different.
Second, West German economic policy toward East Germany was not intended to facilitate German reunification. Given the weight of the cold war,
it is not plausible that the prospects of reunification entered into West
German calculations when West Germany sought to expand economic relations with East Germany. Third, intra-German trade could not and did
not have any significant effects on the basic security relationship between
the two Germanys, although it may have helped reduce uncertainty and
promote mutual understanding. During the cold war, the two Germanys
were critical to the global balance of power between the two superpowers,
and it is unrealistic to think that intra-German trade could have had any
meaningful effect on the global balance of power and, thus, the threat of
war in Germany.

West German economic policy toward East Germany was not motivated
by reunification and security concerns. Instead, its basic goal was to use its
economic power as an instrument of political influence. Although West
Germany could not use that leverage in high politics (e.g., changing the
balance of power in Europe), it had been successful in obtaining some
political concessions from East Germany, such as the release of East German
political prisoners. To induce the asymmetric intra-German economic relationship for political advantage, West Germany provided massive subsidies
to promote economic exchanges with East Germany.

South Korea, like West Germany, should expand intra-Korea economic
exchanges as an instrument of political influence. South Korea must recog-

nize, however, the lessons of the German experience. First, unlike the divided Germany, South Korea must deal with the possible adverse effects of intra-Korea economic cooperation on the delicate military balance of power in the divided Korea. The threat of war on the Korean peninsula cannot be taken lightly in the post–cold war environment. Thus, South Korea must seek an arms control agreement as intra-Korean trade expands; otherwise, North Korea may use the benefits from expanded economic cooperation with South Korea to strengthen its military capabilities. Second, it is doubtful that prereunification economic cooperation under the current environment will significantly affect the cost of eventual economic reunification, although it could if North Korea adopts meaningful economic and political reform. But when North Korea implements such reforms, Korea will have passed the preparation stage and be entering the period of actual reunification.

After reunification, the bulk of public expenditure will be devoted to restructuring North Korean industries. A study by the Korea Development Institute estimates that 50 percent of government expenditure will go to upgrading North Korea's infrastructure.[5] The German experience, however, shows that Korea may not be able to channel as many resources into productive use as it hopes. In 1992, Germany spent only one-fourth of its public expenditure on productive investment; the rest went to social welfare.[6]

The cost of reunification will depend not only on the amount of investment but also on the efficiency of investment spending. The problems and challenges that Germany faced in its efforts to improve the infrastructure in the East provide valuable lessons to Korea.[7]

Planning for the economic development of North Korea in a unified Korea also requires a historical perspective. That is, it is necessary to examine the role that North Korea played in the East Asian regional economy before Korea was divided in 1945. That, in turn, was shaped by Japan's colonial design of the East Asian regional economy. The Japanese development strategy centered around a network of infrastructure that they built in North Korea and Manchuria. In developing infrastructure, the Japanese relied on a unique form of public-private partnership, such as the South Manchurian Railroad Company.[8] As Foster-Carter (1992) aptly observes, public-private cooperation will play an important role in managing the cost of postreunification reconstruction. As South Korea's reputation as Korea, Inc., suggests, it will be in a good position to meet this challenge.

Economic Consequences
of German Reunification

Reunification has imposed a heavy burden on the government budget in Germany. Net government transfers to the new *Lander* were around 140 billion deutsche marks in 1991 and 180 billion deutsche marks in 1992. About one-quarter went to investment; the rest was spent on social welfare and subsidies; 180 billion deutsche marks represents more than 6 percent of gross national product (GNP) and roughly a quarter of total public spending. Big transfers to the new *Lander* are not likely to be temporary. Some suggest that western Germany will have to transfer to eastern Germany a minimum of 100 billion deutsche marks a year for at least the next ten years.[9]

As a result of new government spending in eastern Germany, the total public-spending deficit was close to 200 billion deutsche marks in 1992. If unity spending continues at the projected levels, Germany's stock of public debt could soar to 1.8 trillion deutsche marks, or more than 51 percent of GNP by 1995. Continued public borrowing would have adverse economic consequences, such as high interest rates and trade deficits. If public spending does not abate, Germany will have to undergo the painful adjustment of spending cuts and tax hikes.

The actual cost of reunification in Germany surprises most observers, showing, as it does, the severity of the economic collapse in the new *Lander* after unity. By all accounts, the East German economy has experienced a depression. In the first few months after the economic and monetary union of July 1990, industrial output fell to 60 percent of the average of the first six months of 1990. By the end of the year it was down to 49 percent, and during 1991 it fell to a third of its former level. Even the gross domestic product, which is much less sensitive than industrial output, fell by 35 percent.

The effective unemployment rate rose from almost zero at the beginning of 1990 to 7.2 percent in July of that year and to 25 percent by the spring of 1991. By the end of 1991 it had reached 30 percent. These figures understate the unemployment problem because they include the unemployed workers taking part in job-creation schemes and retraining programs and because "short-time" workers are counted as full-time equivalents. Around 700,000 people who had taken early retirement up to the end of 1991, and around 540,000 commuters who found work in West Germany, are not included in the unemployment figures. By the end of 1991 the total number of persons employed in East Germany had fallen from 9.3–9.7 million to approximately 6 million; as of early summer 1992, East German effective full-time employment was no more than 5 million.[10]

The transition to a market economy entails the inevitable cost of economic adjustment. Four fundamental economic problems of a communist planned economy make its collapse likely when it is integrated into the world economy; they are wrong incentives, wrong institutions, lack of know-how, and wrong prices. Thus, all socialist economies will experience a difficult transition to a market economy.

Reduced demand for East German goods at home and abroad after economic union illustrates the difficulty of economic transition. Once West German products were available, East German consumers chose not to buy uncompetitive East German products, whose shoddiness made them difficult to sell. East German producers also lost their export markets. Before the Council of Mutual Economic Assistance (Comecon or CEMA) collapsed, about two-thirds of East Germany's exports had gone to Comecon countries.

The East German experience, however, was particularly severe, even compared with other East European countries. This observation, however, begs the question of whether better policy might have made a difference in making the East German transition to a market economy more smooth and less costly. The answer seems to be affirmative.

First, the East German economy was integrated into the world economy too quickly. Unlike other East European countries, the institutions of a market economy were introduced to East Germany immediately, without any adjustment period. After the fall of the Berlin Wall in November 1989, only six months elapsed before economic union. Economists differ over the proper speed of reform, but there is no doubt that, at least in the short run, the effects of a big bang approach are likely to be severe. Because policy makers had some control over the timing of economic union in Germany, it is necessary to examine the political debate leading up to Chancellor Helmut Kohl's offer of economic union on February 7, 1990.

Second, the German government took a hands-off policy as East German wages rapidly rose, although it had more control over the level of wages. East German wages after unity have been above market-clearing and full-employment levels, creating the price-cost squeeze that made most East German firms unviable.[11]

Between the first quarter of 1990 and July 1990, average industrial wages per full-time worker rose almost 23 percent. Between July and October 1990, industrial wages rose 16 percent uniformly across industries. The wage increases in other sectors were comparable: for example, between July and October 1990, wages increased 17 percent in mining, 21 percent in wholesale trade, 12 percent in retail trade, and 22 percent in insurance. These increases have narrowed the gap between West and East German wages. In January 1991 construction workers were granted increases that brought their wages to 60 percent of West German levels, and in April 1991 their wages rose to 65 percent of West German levels. In general, the hourly gross wage in the East German manufacturing industry in early 1992 was 50 percent below the West German level but 600 percent above the level of only two years earlier. In the metal industry wage agreement of March 1, 1991, which set the standard for other wage contracts, it was decided that the base wage rates will be adjusted to West German levels by 1994 and that all additional benefits will be adjusted by the following year (Sinn and Sinn 1992, 153). There were also reductions in working hours negotiated in most contracts, with a forty-hour workweek guaranteed in many contracts signed in August.[12]

Third, the recovery of the East German economy has been hampered by the slow progress of privatizing state-run companies in East Germany.

> Between 6,000 and 7,000 industrial combines had to be privatized. Each of these combines had to be broken up into a large number of individual firms—in all, 40,000 separate plants. There were also 45,000 hotels, restaurants, and sales outlets to be dealt with.
>
> As of March 1992, the task of selling or leasing the pharmacies, restaurants, department stores, and shops had been effectively completed. Selling the industrial firms, however, had been proceeding more slowly, specially since the "pearls" were disposed early on. . . . Up to the fall of 1992 (a year after reunification) barely a quarter of the firms originally supervised by the Treuhand had been sold, and by the end of 1992 (18 months after the sales began) the proportion of firms sold may have amounted to about 30 percent.[13]

The consequences of privatization on the cost of reunification and East German employment were severe. The sale of firms up to the end of 1991 was expected to bring in only 100 billion deutsche marks—that is, about one-tenth of the 1 trillion deutsche marks needed to bring capital intensity in the East up to Western levels.

About 1 million jobs were secured through privatization up to the spring of 1992. However, that figure only represented one-tenth of the potential East German workforce, or about one-quarter of the former Treuhand (a government agency) jobs. More than 1.5 million jobs had also disappeared from the statistics of the Treuhand, not by way of privatization but through bankruptcies and dismissals.

Three main policies contributed to the high cost of German reunification: (1) the speed of reunification, which was accelerated by Kohl's offer of economic union on February 7, 1990, (2) a combination of wage policies that led to high wages in East Germany (e.g., currency conversion rate, the introduction of West German institutions of industrial relations, and post-unity labor policy), and (3) an ineffective privatization policy.

Domestic Politics and the
Terms of German Reunification

THE SPEED OF THE REUNIFICATION PROCESS

When the border was opened in November 1989, most people could not have predicted the speed of the developments that led to economic union in July 1990 and to full reunification in October 1990. A key development that set the pace of reunification was Chancellor Kohl's offer of economic union between West and East Germany. Before Kohl's decision, there had been an intense domestic debate in West Germany on reunification.[14]

The debate over reunification began when Kohl presented a ten-point plan for reunification on November 13, 1989. Its main elements were as follows:

- Undertaking joint projects with a view to reducing pollution, improving the railway system, and modernizing the telecommunications system in East Germany
- Establishing linkages in all areas of public life based on intergovernmental treaties after free elections had taken place in East Germany
- Developing confederate structures between West and East Germany
- Creating a West-East German confederation in the context of European integration and in line with the Helsinki agreements on human rights.[15]

Although Kohl's plan signaled West Germany's intention of pursuing reunification, it was based on a gradual approach to reunification through cooperation and preparation. On February 7, 1990, however, Kohl reversed his policy, proposing an economic union to introduce the deutsche mark as the official medium of exchange in East Germany.

Kohl may have abandoned his ten-point plan in favor of immediate reunification because he had no other choice. First, the specter of disintegration in East Germany loomed after the border was opened.[16] News of government paralysis was common. East German premier Hans Modrow confided to Kohl that his orders were not being followed. Because no East German leader had been able to satisfy people's escalating demands for social and economic change, the burden of stabilizing the East German situation fell on the shoulders of West Germany's policy makers.

East Germans showed their dissatisfaction by migrating to West Germany. After some 344,000 East Germans moved west in 1989, emigration continued at a rate of 1,500 to 3,000 a day in January 1990. The only way to persuade East Germans to stay home was to give them some hope of orderly progress toward reunification. In the face of continuing migration, Kohl could not choose a gradual approach, keeping East Germany as a separate economy and using exchange rate policy to protect its domestic and external markets.

Second, Kohl had to make fast progress in internal economic integration so as to make reunification a fait accompli to foreign detractors—mainly, the Soviet Union. After all, the international situation in 1989 provided a historic opportunity for German reunification.[17] The Soviets had lost the will to maintain an external empire and were preoccupied with internal reform. The communist system had collapsed throughout Eastern Europe. Around January 1990, however, Germans were not certain whether the Soviets would accept the North Atlantic Treaty Organization (NATO) membership of a unified Germany, which both West Germany and its Western allies, including the United States, wanted. Accelerating internal economic integration was part of Kohl's strategy, in cooperation with the United States, to present German reunification as an irreversible process.

Third, Kohl had to respond to East Germans' demands for swift reunification. As early as in mid-November 1989, street demonstrators—first in Leipzig and then numerous other municipalities—began to chant for national reunification. East Germans voted for the Christian Democratic Party (CDU)-led conservative coalition in the March 18, 1990, election because the CDU supported swift reunification.

There is, however, evidence that those three factors did not necessarily make immediate reunification the only option. First, migration from East Germany may not have posed a serious problem even if it had continued. The number of migrants from East Germany each year has never exceeded those of migrants of German origin from other East European countries. Also, the West German economy was able to absorb migration inflows. The West German unemployment rate actually decreased 0.5 percent between the third quarter of 1989 and July 1990, despite the surge in migration during that time.

In addition, a great majority of East Germans were reluctant to migrate. A survey showed that 75 percent of usually mobile East German university students preferred to stay in East Germany and were willing to take eastern jobs that might pay less than half of those in the West.

Second, the German public, especially East Germans, may not have uniformly supported immediate reunification. Public opinion data from various sources show that Germans somewhat reluctantly supported swift and comprehensive reunification. The strong push for reunification by the political leadership was not a response to grassroots sentiments but the contrary: the public followed its leaders.[18]

Third, economic union may not have been necessary to win Soviet support for German reunification. Mikhail Gorbachev's main concern was the alliance status of a new Germany. He accepted German reunification in principle in late January 1990, days before Kohl proposed economic union.

More plausibly, Kohl may have accelerated the reunification process to strengthen his domestic political base. After the 1987 election, in which the CDU retained its majority, its popularity began to decline. A series of political scandals and declining economic conditions decreased popular support for the the CDU, which was also challenged by a new conservative party, the Republicans. Championing a more conservative and nationalist program, the Republicans made inroads into the Christian Democrats' voting base. Public opinion polls at the time showed that the CDU was vulnerable to a strong electoral challenge by the opposition parties.[19] In late 1989, Kohl's party was trailing in the polls and his personal image as a leader was badly tarnished. Because 1990 was an election year (the Basic Law required that a federal election be held in late 1990 or early 1991), unfolding events in East Germany made reunification an election issue and major parties in West Germany committed themselves to one or another reunification policy. Kohl's announcement came in this context.[20]

West German leaders initially hesitated to intervene in developments in East Germany because West Germany had recognized the East German state as a cooperation partner. West German governments after Social Democratic Party (SPD) chancellor Willy Brandt recognized East Germany as a separate state and sought to expand cooperation between the two Germanys.

When it became clear that a continued relationship with the East German government was a liability, West German political leaders distanced themselves from it and sought to extend their influence directly to East Germany. Their political competition in East Germany intensified when East German prime minister Modrow scheduled an election for March 18, 1990. In this battle to win East German voters, Kohl had three advantages over his competitors. First, his party had historically been a proreunification party. Second, his party had the right message; ex post, swift reunification was what East German voters demanded. Third, his main opponent, the SPD, was divided.

The CDU began to portray itself as the party of unity in mid 1989. Although the CDU had accepted the principles of *Ostpolitik* (such as recognizing the legitimacy of the East German state, the primacy of dialogue, and East Germany's capacity for reform), it had given higher priority to reunification than did the SPD, the architect of *Ostpolitik*. The Christian Democrats refused to give in on basic principles such as the existence of a single German citizenship.[21]

Kohl, with a simple and unified position for East German voters, moved on several fronts to prepare for the March 1990 general elections in East Germany. He consolidated the East German conservative parties (the CDU-East, the Democratic Awakening, and the German Social Union) into a single coalition, Alliance for Germany. In so doing, Kohl created an image of a new organization, one not associated with the past. Kohl also persuaded the CDU-East to accept East German accession to the Federal Republic under Article 23 of West Germany's Basic Law. (The East German Christian Democrats were initially undecided between Article 23 and Article 146. Article 146 would have required the drafting of a new constitution for Germany by a popularly chosen constitutional assembly.) Through this process, Kohl's party developed a sharp and unified message for a swift and procedurally simple reunification.

The SPD at the time was also divided. Willy Brandt embraced German unity as a natural development, but its then leader, Oskar Lafontaine, continued to resist reunification. Lafontaine appealed to West German taxpayers' discontent about having to bankroll East German migrants immediately and a rise in East Germany's standard of living later. Still, other Social Democrats, fearing that their party would repeat history and again alienate voters by an antinational stance, proposed even faster confederation than Kohl was proposing.

During the campaign for the March 1990 East German election, the West German Social Democrats generally favored Article 146 (over Article 23), arguing for a slow process that would keep the East German identity separate during the transition period. The left-wing leader of the SPD-East, Inrahim Bohme, agreed, although his party members were split on the issue. East German voters, however, saw the choice as black and white. The Social Democrats also hurt their chances by targeting conservatives rather than the hated communists as their primary opponents and by the constant disparagement of reunification by West German chancellor candidate Lafontaine.[22]

THE LEVEL OF WAGES IN EAST GERMANY—
COLLECTIVE BARGAINING AND
THE CURRENCY CONVERSION RATE

Some of the factors that contributed to high wages in East Germany were economic, as East German workers migrated to West Germany, while capital moved in the opposite direction. Another observer, however, downplayed that theory because wages rose rapidly in contrast to the slow movements of migration and investment. Another hypothesis is that the wage increases were partly intended to compensate workers for higher payroll deductions and the elimination of price subsidies.

Wage increases in East Germany were also affected by the one-to-one conversion rate chosen for East German wage contracts. Survey results show that a majority of East German workers believe that the conversion rate contributed to the rise of their wages. That wages rose despite the favorable conversion rate, however, casts doubt on the significance of the conversion rate. Unions, whose goal was parity between East and West German wages, may have succeeded in bringing wages to the current level, regardless of their initial level.

But these economic factors are not sufficient to account for the actual size of wage increases. The consensus appears to be that the main cause of wage increases was union bargaining power in East Germany.[23] Bargaining power is a relative concept, and union successes in East Germany reflect union strength or management weakness or both. East German workers were well organized even before formal economic union. Throughout the spring of 1990, the individual unions of the western Confederation of German Trade Unions (DGB) negotiated cooperative agreements with their eastern counterparts. After individual East German industrial unions abandoned their peak association, the Free German Trade Union Federation (FDGB) and the DGB stepped in to fill the void. To make a clean break with the past, the DGB rejected any formal merger with the eastern federation or any of its component unions. Instead, the western unions individually enrolled eastern workers into their unions. During 1990, 3.6 million members from East Germany joined the DGB. By the beginning of 1991, the DGB unions already represented 40 percent of the eastern labor force. (The corresponding number for West Germany is about 40 percent.)[24]

In contrast, management was in disarray. The main employer in East Germany was the Treuhand, whose officials could not represent the interests of existing capital because it was not their capital that was at stake. A large proportion of East German managers from the previous regime remained. They were unaccustomed to collective bargaining and knew that they would ultimately lose their jobs, no matter how wage agreements were negotiated.

The situation did not change when the West German employers' associations participated in the negotiations beginning in the fall of 1990. West German management had little incentive to resist wage demands because low wages threatened not only West German workers but West German capital. East German workers did not have an incentive to moderate their demands because their unemployment benefits depended on the size of their last salary.

The German government did not intervene to rein in wage increases, perhaps because of its traditional aloof policy. In the face of mounting criticism, however, the German government began intervening belatedly in 1993. As part of the "solidarity pact," Kohl was able to gain some concessions from trade unions in 1993. In the opening negotiations for the 1993 wage contracts, unions demanded only half the 10 percent rise that they had asked for in 1992.[25] East German companies gave even lower wages and, in some cases, were able to break existing wage agreements.

Privatization

Criticisms of the Treuhand abounded, mostly directed at its management problems. The Treuhand was accused of favoring German investors. Other frequent complaints were that the Treuhand was slow or uninterested in selling small firms because of its emphasis on speed. Of course, the slow progress in privatization may have been exacerbated by the inability of the capital markets to absorb the properties on sale. Some recognize, however, that the Treuhand's tasks were difficult. It was supposed not only to sell but to reconstruct or close down. Alternatives might be auctioning off firms or decentralizing.

The most difficult problem in the early days of operation were disputes over property rights. No less than 2 million compensation claims have been made, among which were 11,200 claims for the return of firms. Natural restitution carried out through the municipal authorities has proved to be a complete failure. By October 1991 only about 3.3 percent of the claims had been settled; 90 percent of the decisions regarding the restitution of firms were being contested and were thus not yet legally valid.

The problem arose from the West German decision to extend natural restitution to former owners as a part of economic union. As a result, the Treuhand did not have clear title to all its holdings. Properties expropriated after the establishment of East Germany at the end of the Soviet occupation could be claimed by their original owners, as could properties taken between 1933 and 1945 for religious and political reasons. Monetary compensation to former owners would have eased the problem. But the treaty made it clear that the former owners had greater rights. A legal claim made by a previous owner prevented the disposal of the disputed property and allowed a great deal of pressure to be exercised.

According to the chief West German negotiator, Wolfgang Schauble, the preference for restitution over indemnity in property claims was specified in the June 15, 1990, bilateral statement preceding economic union, at the insistence of the Free Democratic Party, the Christian Social Union, and one section of the Christian Democratic Union, in part to minimize the government's financial burden. (In retrospect, Schauble says that he would have changed the restitution rule in favor of indemnity.) During the negotiations, the East German government favored financial compensation for dispossessed property owners because it wanted to facilitate new investment and to keep as much as possible of the value of the state-owned businesses for the East German people.

The German Experience and the Political Economy of Korean Reunification

The German experience shows that politicizing the reunification process can be costly. But it also shows that reunification does not have to be expensive if appropriate policies are chosen. I argue that Korean reunification will proceed without the problems of German reunification because Korean policy makers, relatively free of domestic political pressure, will be able to choose appropriate policies.

First, Korean policy makers will be able to keep the North a separate state for the time being. As the German experience shows, the flow of migration may not be an insurmountable problem; like East German workers, North Koreans may also be reluctant to leave. South Korea's continuing labor shortages mean that it can absorb a sizable number of migrants without disrupting its labor market.

Kohl politicized the reunification process because his domestic political position was not secure. Although Korean policy makers may be under political pressure to reunify immediately, gradualism could succeed for the following reasons. First, both North and South Koreans will have learned that quick reunification can do a lot of harm and not demand it. Second, unlike Kohl, a South Korean leader will have a secure domestic power base. If the current reform program under President Kim Young-sam succeeds without dividing the dominant conservative voting bloc, there is a distinct possibility for one-party dominance in South Korea.

Despite their electoral security, leaders of the South Korean ruling party may be tempted to politicize the reunification process if the opposition parties try to gain the advantage in North Korea. But if the German experience is any indication, North Koreans will vote for the ruling South Korean party. The dominant South Korean party will thus have the upper hand and be able to shape the course of reunification.

The success of gradualism, however, depends on policy makers' demonstrating their commitment to reunification and to the welfare of North Koreans. Thus, once South Korea has had a chance to shape the course of reunification, it should announce a clear timetable and commit itself to it; using 1992 as a target date had great symbolic importance to the success of European integration. South Korean policy makers must ensure that politicians do not promise North Koreans more than they can deliver and that North Koreans do not suffer from Southern "carpetbaggers."

Second, Korean policy makers will be better able to manage wage levels in North Korea. Even if the current labor laws are extended to North Korea and South Korean unions are allowed to organize North Korean counterparts, the Korean state will still be able to dominate industrial relations. A rapid decline in strike activity after 1990 attests to the influence of the state in Korean industrial relations.[26]

The power of the Korean labor movement may grow as democratization in South Korea continues. The new Kim Young-sam government may revise the labor laws in favor of labor, which will undoubtedly invigorate the Korean labor movement. But Korean labor is unlikely to reach the status of West German labor in the domestic polity. The power of West German trade unions—having won for their members the world's highest pay and some of the shortest working hours—is unique even among developed countries.

A pessimistic outlook for labor's political power is based on its electoral weakness. In Korean electoral politics, class is not an important electoral cleavage. In the 1992 National Assembly election, voters' income and occupation did not significantly affect their party choice. Among 159 blue-collar workers surveyed by Chan Wook Park, only 32.7 percent voted for the opposition party most sympathetic to the labor movement, whereas 44.0 percent supported the Democratic Liberal Party, the government party at the time.[27]

Third, Korean policy makers will be able to solve the problem of property rights in North Korea. There is no doubt that, once reunification is within reach, many South Koreans of North Korean origin (more than five million North Koreans migrated to South Korea before and during the Korean War) will seek the return of their real estate. There are already many legal disputes over the land inside the demilitarized zone.

However, the dispute over property rights may not be a serious one in Korea. South Korean citizens have been unable to mount any organized resistance to the government's expropriating land for construction projects or zoning restrictions in the greenbelt. Even as South Korea democratizes, there is little evidence that the state's ability to restrict the exercise of property rights is being challenged. Finally, a political party like Germany's FDP, which champions the primacy of free market and individual property rights, does not exist in South Korea.

Conclusion

The high cost of German reunification has had a chilling effect on Korea's hopes for reunification. Many openly question the necessity of reunification, fearing the high cost. This fear, however, is unjustified. The high cost of Germany's reunification was the product of its domestic political dynamic, and Korea does not have to repeat the German experience. In particular, as this chapter has argued, Korea will be able to avoid three major German policy mistakes—the speed and timing of economic unity, the hands-off wage policy in East Germany after union, and the decision to restore property rights to the former owners of East German properties.

Although a one-sided merger, if controlled, does not have to be costly, it will by no means be easy. The most difficult problem will be minimizing the politicization of the reunification process, that is, protecting North Koreans from demagogues taking advantage of North Koreans' difficult adjustment or carpetbaggers looking to exploit North Koreans' economic vulnerability.

In particular, Korean policy makers must prepare for political opposition when they try to pace the process toward economic union. There will be strong nationalistic, moral, and political pressure for immediate economic union. To diffuse such pressure, Korean policy makers must demonstrate their commitment to economic union while keeping the pace carefully controlled. Thus, I recommend that in the beginning stages of the process, Korean policy makers affirm the general objective of economic union, announce a target date, and list the preparatory measures that will need to be enacted. Detailed legislation will take place in future negotiations and consultations. What I propose is the equivalent of the Single European Act of 1985, which set 1992 as the target date to complete the single market in Europe.

Notes

I would like to thank Susanne Lohmann and Frank P. Wardlaw for their comments.

1. I draw on the extensive literature on the economics of German reunification. See, for example, Leslie Lipschitz and Donogh McDonald, "Introduction and Overview," in Lipschitz and McDonald, eds., *German Unification: Economic Issues*, Occasional Paper 75 (Washington, D.C.: International Monetary Fund, 1990);

George A. Akerlof et al., "East Germany in from the Cold: The Economic Aftermath of Currency Union," *Brookings Papers on Economic Activity* 1(1991):1-105; Manfred J. M. Neumann, "German Unification: Economic Problems and Consequences" (Paper delivered at the Carnegie-Rochester Conference on Public Policy, April 19–20, 1991); A. Chanie Ghaussy and Wolf Schafer, eds., *The Economics of German Unification* (London and New York: Routledge, 1993).

2. Albert O. Hirschman, "Exit, Voice and the Fate of the German Democratic Republic: An Essay in Conceptual History," *World Politics* 45(1993):173–202.

3. Sang Man Lee, "Prospects for North-South Korean Economic Cooperation" (in Korean), *Korean Journal of Unification Affairs* 5, no. 1 (1993):90-128; Hacheong Yeon, *Practical Means to Improve Intra-Korea Trade and Economic Cooperation*, KDI Working Paper, no.9301 (Seoul: Korea Development Institute, 1993).

4. Il-dong Koh, "Development of Intra-German Economic Relations and North-South Korean Economic Cooperation" (in Korean), *Korean Journal of Unification Affairs* 5, no. 1 (1993):234–59.

5. Shim Jae Hoon, "The Price of Unity," *Far Eastern Economic Review*, March 26, 1992, p. 56.

6. "Germany: Shock of Unity," *The Economist*, May 23, 1992, p. 3.

7. Herbert Baum, "Transport Policy in Eastern Germany," in Ghaussy and Schafer, eds., *The Economics of German Unification*, pp. 155–76.

8. Ramon H. Myers, "Japanese Imperialism in Manchuria: The South Manchuria Railroad Company, 1906–1933," in Peter Duus, Ramon H. Myers, and Mark R. Peattie, eds., *The Japanese Informal Empire in China, 1895–1987* (Princeton, N.J.: Princeton University Press, 1989).

9. The statement of Kurt Biedenkopf, premier of Saxony, as reported in "Germany: Shock of Unity," *The Economist*, May 23, 1992, p. 5.

10. The unemployment figures only weakly reflect the sharp decline in production because emigration, early retirement, and massive subsidies given to East German industry by the Treuhand reduced the number of workers looking for jobs in East Germany. See Gerlinde Sinn and Hans-Werner Sinn, *Jumpstart: The Economic Unification of Germany* (Cambridge, Mass.: MIT Press, 1992).

11. Akerlof et al., "East Germany in from the Cold," pp. 1–105.

12. Ibid., p. 56, and Sinn and Sinn, *Jumpstart*, p. 153.

13. Sinn and Sinn, *Jumpstart*, pp. 82–83.

14. For a general introduction to West German domestic politics, see Peter J. Katzenstein, *Policy and Politics in West Germany* (Philadelphia, Pa.: Temple University Press, 1987). For detailed descriptions of the events leading up to German reunification, see Peter H. Merkl, *German Unification in the European Context* (University Park: Pennsylania State University Press, 1993); Elizabeth Pond, *Beyond the Wall: Germany's Road to Unification* (Washington, D.C.: Brookings Institution, 1993); and A. James McAdams, *Germany Divided: From the Wall to Reunification* (Princeton, N.J.: Princeton University Press, 1993). See also Karl Kaiser, "Germany's Unification," *Foreign Affairs* 70(1991):179–205, and Barbara Lippert et al., *German*

Unification and EC Integration (New York: Council of Foreign Relations Press, 1993), for the international dimension of German reunification. I have relied on all these sources for my account of the reunification process.

15. Thomas Mayer and Gunther Thumann, "German Democratic Republic: Background and Plans for Reform," in Lipschitz and McDonald, eds., *German Unification: Economic Issues,* p. 50.

16. For an analysis of the regime collapse in East Germany with a focus on the role of collective action by private citizens, see Hirschman, "Exit, Voice and the Fate of the German Democratic Republic," and Susanne Lohmann, "The Dynamics of Regime Collapse: The Monday Demonstrations in Leipzig, East Germany, 1989–1991," Graduate School of Business Research Paper no. 1225, Stanford University, 1993.

17. For the international dimension of German reunification, see Kaiser, "Germany's Unification," and Lippert et al., *German Unification.*

18. Akerlof et al., "East Germany in from the Cold," pp. 49–55, and Manfred Kuechler, "The Road to German Unity: Mass Sentiment in East and West Germany," *Public Opinion Quarterly* 56(1992):53–75.

19. Russell J. Dalton, *Politics in Germany* (New York: HarperCollins, 1993), p. 290.

20. In a personal correspondence (December 30, 1993), Frank P. Wardlaw comments that Kohl also faced pressure from strong German exile groups in his own party who favored quick reunification.

21. McAdams, *Germany Divided,* p. 215.

22. Pond, *Beyond the Wall,* p. 198.

23. For an explanation of the postunion transformation of labor markets and industrial relations in East Germany, see Sinn and Sinn, *Jumpstart;* Akerlof et al., "East Germany in from the Cold," pp. 59–64; Christoph F. Buechtemann and Juergen Schupp, "Repercussions of Reunification: Patterns and Trends in the Socio-Economic Transformation of East Germany," *Industrial Relations Journal* 23(1992):90–106; Ulrich Jurgens et al., "The Transformation of Industrial Relations in East Germany," *Industrial and Labor Relations Review* 46(1993):229–44; Alan B. Krueger and Jorn-Steffen Pischke, "A Comparative Analysis of East and West German Labor Markets: Before and After Unification," Working Paper no. 4154 (Washington, D.C.: National Bureau of Economic Research, 1992); and Wolfgang Streeck, "More Uncertainties: German Unions Facing 1992," *Industrial Relations* 30(1991):317–49.

24. Dalton, *Politics in Germany,* p. 242.

25. "Germany Labours On," *The Economist,* January 23, 1993, pp. 63–64. See also "Otherwise Engaged," *The Economist,* June 20, 1992, pp. 64–66, and "Privatising East Germany," *The Economist,* September 1991, pp. 21–24, on the Treuhand and the transition.

26. Jongryn Mo, "Democratization and the South Korean State: Management of Industrial Relations, 1987–1992" (Manuscript, University of Texas at Austin, November 1993).

27. Chan Wook Park, "Pattern of Party Support in the 14th National Assembly Election" (in Korean) (Manuscript, Seoul National University, 1992).

References

Akerlof, George A., et al. "East Germany in from the Cold: The Economic Aftermath of Currency Union." *Brookings Papers on Economic Activity*, no. 1 (1991):1–105.

Baum, Herbert. "Transport Policy in Eastern Germany." In *The Economics of German Unification*, ed. A. Ghanie Ghaussy and Wolf Schafer. London and New York: Routledge, 1993.

Buechtemann, Christoph F., and Juergen Schupp. "Repercussions of Reunification: Patterns and Trends in the Socio-Economic Transformation of East Germany." *Industrial Relations Journal* 23(1992):90–106.

Dalton, Russell J. *Politics in Germany.* New York: HarperCollins, 1993.

Foster-Carter, Aidan. *Korea's Coming Unification: Another East Asian Superpower?* Special Report no. M212, The Economist Intelligence Unit, 1992.

Hasse, Rolf. "German-German Monetary Union: Many Options, Costs and Repercussions." In *The Economics of German Unification*, ed. A. Ghanie Ghaussy and Wolf Schafer. London and New York: Routledge, 1993.

Hirschman, Albert O. "Exit, Voice, and the Fate of the German Democratic Republic: An Essay in Conceptual History." *World Politics* 45(1993):173–202.

Jurgens, Ulrich, Larissa Klinzing, and Lowell Turner. "The Transformation of Industrial Relations in East Germany." *Industrial and Labor Relations Review* 46 (1993):229–44.

Kaiser, Karl. "Germany's Unification." *Foreign Affairs* 70(1991):179–205.

Katzenstein, Peter J. *Policy and Politics in West Germany.* Philadelphia, Pa.: Temple University Press. 1987.

———. "Industry in a Changing West Germany." In *Industry and Politics in West Germany*, ed. Peter J. Katzenstein. Ithaca, N.Y.: Cornell University Press, 1989.

Koh, Il-dong. "Development of Intra-German Economic Relations and North-South Korean Economic Cooperation" (in Korean). *Korean Journal of Unification Affairs* 5, no. 1(1993):234–59.

Kreile, Michael. "The Political Economy of the New Germany." In *The New Germany and the New Europe*, ed. Paul B. Stares. Washington, D.C.: Brookings Institution, 1992.

Krueger, Alan B., and Jorn-Steffen Pischke. "A Comparative Analysis of East and West German Labor Markets: Before and after Unification." Working Paper no. 4154, National Bureau of Economic Research, 1992.

Kuechler, Manfred. "The Road to German Unity: Mass Sentiment in East and West Germany." *Public Opinion Quarterly* 56(1992):53–76.

Lee, Sang Man. "Prospects for North-South Korean Economic Cooperation" (in Korean). *Korean Journal of Unification Affairs* 5, no.1(1993):90–128.

Lippert, Barbara, Rosalind Stevens-Strohmann, Dirk Gunter, Grit Viertel, and Stephen Woolcock. *German Unification and EC Integration*. New York: Council of Foreign Relations Press, 1993.

Lipschitz, Leslie. "Introduction and Overview." In *German Unification: Economic Issues*, ed. Leslie Lipschitz and Donogh McDonald. Occasional Paper 75, International Monetary Fund, 1993.

Lohmann, Susanne. "The Dynamics of Regime Collapse: The Monday Demonstrations in Leipzig, East Germany, 1989–1991." Graduate School of Business Research Paper no. 1225, Stanford University, 1993.

McAdams, A. James. *Germany Divided: From the Wall to Reunification*. Princeton, N.J.: Princeton University Press, 1993.

Mayer, Thomas, and Gunther Thumann. "German Democratic Republic: Background and Plans for Reform." In *German Unification: Economic Issues.*, ed. Leslie Lipschitz and Donogh McDonald. Occasional Paper 75, International Monetary Fund, 1990.

Merkl, Peter H. *German Unification in the European Context*. University Park: Pennsylvania State University Press, 1992.

Mo, Jongryn. "Democratization and the South Korean State: Management of Industrial Relations, 1987–1992." Manuscript, University of Texas at Austin, November 1993.

Myers, Ramon H. "Japanese Imperialism in Manchuria: The South Manchuria Railroad Company, 1906–1933." In *The Japanese Informal Empire in China, 1895–1987*, ed. Peter Duus, Ramon H. Myers, and Mark R. Peattie. Princeton, N.J.: Princeton University Press, 1989.

Neumann, Manfred J. M. "German Unification: Economic Problems and Consequences." Paper delivered at Carnegie-Rochester Conference on Public Policy, April 19–20, 1991.

Park, Chan Wook. "Pattern of Party Support in the 14th National Assembly Election" (in Korean). Manuscript, Seoul National University, 1992.

Pond, Elizabeth. *Beyond the Wall: Germany's Road to Unification*. Washington, D.C.: Brookings Institution, 1993.

Sinn, Gerlinde, and Hans-Werner Sinn. *Jumpstart: The Economic Unification of Germany*. Cambridge, Mass.: MIT Press, 1992.

Streeck, Wolfgang. "More Uncertainties: German Unions Facing 1992." *Industrial Relations* 30(1991):317–49.

Thelen, Kathleen A. *Unions of Parts: Labor Politics in Postwar Germany*. Ithaca, N.Y.:Cornell University Press, 1991.

Turner, Lowell. *Democracy at Work: Changing World Markets and the Future of Labor Unions*. Ithaca, N.Y.: Cornell University Press, 1991.

Yeon, Ha-cheong. *Practical Means to Improve Intra-Korea Trade and Economic Cooperation*. KDI Working Paper no. 9301. Seoul, Korea: Korea Development Institute, 1993.

4

Political Leadership, Vision, and Korean Reunification

Thomas H. Henriksen

Korean reunification requires a Korean brand of political leadership and vision that, no doubt, will draw inspiration, if not model and direction, from the kingdom of Silla's absorption of Paekche and Koguryo, which overcame past divisions on the peninsula in the seventh century. The exuberance of Silla's political leadership, infused with its own vibrant brand of culture, led to a single polity on the Korean peninsula that endured to the middle of this century with only brief periods of division. Later, the Koryo dynasty (936–1392), a successor to Silla, forged the borders of what constitutes modern-day Korea. Whereas those early unifications in the dawn of modern Korean history are symbolic precursors to today's challenges, the reunification experiences of other societies in the contemporary world can offer lessons of vision and political leadership for Koreans, despite their far different backgrounds and circumstances.

The convoluted history of the numerous efforts at Korean reunification over the past four decades all but guarantees its singularity. Whether North Korea implodes with a "big bang" or dissipates gradually, its reuniting with the South will severely challenge Korea's political leaders, in the North as well as in the South. Will Korean unification resemble the sudden collapse and reunification in contemporary Germany or the long, painful reconciliation of the postbellum American South? Or will it replicate the far easier reunifications of Vichy France and divided Italy following their partitions of World War II, neither of which required massive adjustments after the Allied victory? The deliberate pace of Yemen's new unity provides another example of the end of communism in one half followed by a unification with the other half to form a single polity. To use modern corporate terms, Germany witnessed an acquisition and Yemen a merger. As such, the overall modes of their reunification differed, even though each had elements similar to the other.

Korea's history, culture, and traditions ensure that recombining North and South may well be sui generis. Several features—the Korean War in the 1950s, the bitter division between the two societies, and Kim Il Sung's rigid, nearly five-decade grip on society above the thirty-eighth parallel, all of which make life there qualitatively different from other communist regimes—guarantee that a reuniting will be fraught with twist and turns. The lingering acrimony from the conflict endures on both sides of the border, but the North officially orchestrates it. The Pyongyang news agency reported that some one and a half million people joined a special army during the "semiwar" period in March 1993, some reportedly signing oaths in blood to fight and die for Kim Il Sung in a "sacred war of reunification."[1] The tremendous gap in living standards and incomes between the two countries also poses a problem. By 1992, the Southerners approached an income of $7,000 per capita; Northerners had an estimated $1,000.[2] To explore the effect that political leadership and vision can have on the reunification process, this essay will examine two pertinent case studies, that of the two Germanys and that of the two Yemens.

Comparisons and Differences, Similarities and Dissimilarities

THE TWO GERMANYS

Comparisons of recent cases of reunification are difficult because the objects being compared vary greatly. The commonality between the most often compared cases under review here—North Korea and the former East Germany—is communism. Their respective population sizes, however, undercut an easy comparison. In 1989, when the Berlin Wall came down, East Germany had about seventeen million people and North Korea about twenty-one million people. But the ratio between the two Koreas is not as favorable as it was between the two Germanys: West Germany had a population of sixty million, whereas South Korea has only some forty-three millon. Thus, West Germany had almost a four to one ratio to the former

East German population, but South Korea has only a two to one ratio with North Korea.

The communist systems in the two states, while sharing similar aspects, still differ markedly. Surrounded by a virtual shell, North Korea is a far more closed society in its totalitarian features than the former East Germany. At the geographic crossroads of Eastern and Western Europe, the two Germanys were often forced together. With West Germany's most important city (Berlin) in the midst of East Germany, the two halves had at times to cooperate despite the Berlin Wall. But, unlike the two Germanys, the two Koreas cannot agree on interstate travel, reciprocal trade, or the exchange of correspondence between separated families. Foreign visitors had far more access to the German Democratic Republic (GDR) than to the Democratic People's Republic of Korea (DPRK). In short, the two Germanys experienced a peaceful coexistence and growing economic cooperation during the decade before reunification. East Germany's collapse and its rejoining West Germany were virtually bloodless, in part because of the peace that had prevailed between the two states during their divided history.

East Germany, along with other communist states to its east, had sympathizers and proponents in the Western world who touted its welfare systems as well as its absence of crime and other social ills of the United States. East Germany's great success in the Olympic Games was often claimed by its proponents to be the earmark of a superior society whose creative energies flowed to sport rather than to capitalistic acquisitiveness—until German athletic prowess was found to be the result of a sports training program that would have been the envy of the ancient Spartans and that relied heavily on drugs, sending shock waves of protest through international sports that reverberate to this day.

Moved as much by their hatred of capitalism and Western bourgeois values as by their love for communism, sympathetic intellectuals served to blunt criticism of Marxism and its embodiment east of the Berlin Wall. They shared some reservations about communist successes in Poland and Hungary but believed that Teutonic efficiency all but guaranteed socialism working well in the GDR. These same academicians, however, never developed any such affinity for North Korea. The DPRK's hermetic seal, its Stalinist aspects, and its avoidance of outside contacts have denied it the same sort of sympathy enjoyed by other communist states such as Cuba, Angola, and Mozambique along with the Soviet Union.

East Germany was dissimilar from North Korea in other ways. A fully industrialized country on a par with West Germany at the end of World War II, East Germany's economy was wrecked by three communist approaches. First, its highly productive agriculture system was replaced by collectivization. Second, its high-grade machinery and aircraft production industries were replaced by heavy industry—iron, steel, and shipbuilding. Third, its infrastructure—railways, buildings, and manufacturing—was not maintained, which was typical of communist practices elsewhere. In contrast, North Korea's industrial development was imposed on a largely agricultural society.

Both the former GDR and the DPRK, however, share dilapidated economic systems that are unresponsive to consumer wants, lagging behind the advanced service economies of the late twentieth century. Just as East Germany requires massive reconstruction, so too will North Korea once it reunites with the Republic of Korea. Although they share this similarity, their respective outcomes await the march of history.

Outside observers often overplay the unity of German culture when considering Germany's reunification from the vantage point of hindsight. This is a mistake, for Germans have demonstrated a remarkable lack of common identity, attributed by scholars to the "profound historical discontinuity in the German experience."[3] Indeed, Germans have fought each other for centuries, often allying with foreigners to fight one another. Even Germany's national unity came much later than other Western countries.[4] Without a strong sense of political continuity or geographic unity, Germans also lack a spiritual coherence. By contrast, the Korean identity is grounded in a long historical process.

Backward communist states becoming prosperous, free-market societies lacks completed case studies. Currently, in East Germany and South Yemen, both of which had communist regimes, new leaders are confronting past authoritarianism and command economies with democratic and free-market systems. These two states must deal with not only socioeconomic transformations but also mergers with their more prosperous and democratic sibling states. They offer not models for Korea but examples of what can happen in different cultural and historical settings.

THE TWO YEMENS

The Yemeni unification, accomplished in May 1990, deserves scrutiny, for it is both a model for emulation and a lesson for caution. The Yemeni unification process itself was a model of rational and accommodative planning and peaceful, orderly execution, defying the stereotypes of the Middle East where conflict, not cooperation, so often characterizes political events. Yet notwithstanding its auspicious and exemplary beginning, the subsequent Yemeni political union has been an uneasy one, erupting into a full-scale war in May 1994.

Britain's advances on the Yemeni peninsula early in this century led to a partition of the region with the declining Ottoman empire. That split fos-

tered two distinct political systems and two different political cultures, each
with its own interests, values, beliefs, and outlooks. South Yemen adopted
a Marxist regime in 1967 with the establishment of the People's Democratic
Republic of Yemen (PDRY) and the winning of independence from Britain.
The North became a republic in 1962 after overthrowing the feudal imamate
but retained its traditional religious and cultural orientation. The years that
followed saw two border wars, in 1972 and 1979, and the South's sponsor-
ship of rebellion against the North. Despite the division and the various
colonial rulers, virtually all Yemenis sought unification. Their motives encompassed sentimental reasons as well as more practical objectives, in that
the principal oil fields bestrode the border. Effective exploitation of the oil
could only be attained through unification and economic integration.

Inter-Yemeni relations opened a new chapter in 1982 with the ending
of the conflict between North and South. The cessation of hostilities brought
discreet economic and sociopolitical steps toward cooperation, fostered by
personal ties between the leaders of the two countries. Six years later, following a border dispute, the two sides dismantled their military positions
and withdrew their forces from the borderlands. Next, the parties worked
out a plan for free movement of citizens and goods over the common border
and linked their two electric power grids. Other steps furthered cooperation,
coordination, and integration, moving the Yemenis toward mutually beneficial relations and paving the way for unification steps by the late 1980s.
By 1986, the impoverished South Yemenis had abandoned Marxist governance after a bloody turmoil within the ruling party. (The North Yemenis
had introduced fledgling multiparty democracy before the transition began.)
Also, the Soviet Union's power had begun to ebb and with it the patronage
of South Yemen, thereby providing a favorable international context for a
merger.[5]

A joint committee, convened in late 1989, hammered out an agreement
that preceded the two Yemens' unification into a new state and polity. The
meeting laid the practical groundwork: Laws, currencies, and income taxes
were standardized; plans were made to merge the two civil services; a joint
constitution was prepared and ratified; and a transitional government operated in Sana for the thirty-month transition period, with a five-member
Presidential Council governing the state. The president was Ali Abdullah
Salih, formerly president of North Yemen; the vice president was Ali Salim
al-Baydh, previously secretary-general of the ruling Yemeni Socialist Party
in the South.

To conciliate the politicians of North and South, the new thirty-nine-
member cabinet accommodated most members of the two former cabinets.
Key portfolios were disbursed to Northerners and Southerners. Likewise,
the House of Representatives (301 members) consisted of members from the

North and South legislative bodies. Lesser officials, as in the new cabinet, were equally distributed to avert tensions during the transition. Before formal unification on May 22, 1990, the military forces along the borders were withdrawn and their units redeployed in other parts of the country, sometimes under commanders from the different regions in what became the Republic of Yemen. Each state's security apparatus was disbanded, and a new one was formed.[6]

The deliberative, even systematic nature of the unification of the two Yemens did not proceed free of hitches or without considerable effort. The Yemenis employed mechanisms for reconciliation through political structures that included Northerners and Southerners. These mechanisms, which ensured the participation of the political elites, included scores of meetings, three joint cabinet sessions, and two hard-bargaining summits between President Salih and Secretary-General al-Baydh. At times the process resembled a halting two steps forward and one step backward movement. Northern leaders, fearing that the regime in Aden was on the verge of collapse, viewed unification as a preventive measure against a more risky military intervention, whereas the Southern leadership's fortunes required a merger to revive their standing. Weakened by the 1986 civil war and riven by continuing factions, the PDRY politicians needed unification for a new lease on their political life.

In the end the transition went forward in a phased, sequential manner. Misgivings among the traditional Northerners, whose devotion to Islam put them at odds with the Southerners' Marxism and secularism, were overcome. The Northerners' fears were somewhat allayed by the demographic balance in their favor (approximately seven million in the North as against less than three million in the South). Not only did the North hold the demographic balance but it had the stronger economy, possessing oil exports, more agriculture potential, and a greater number of expatriates working abroad who sent remittances home.

Postunified Yemen, however, has been marked by political unease despite the success of its reunification process. During 1993, Yemen was racked by factional disputes so characteristic of its past. Banditry reoccurred among its nomadic tribesmen, who became embroiled in local conflicts with foreign oil companies, sometimes taking the nonindigenous workers as hostages. The most celebrated case involved the temporary kidnapping of Haynes Mahoney, an employee with the United States Information Service in Sana.

That seizure of an American official called attention to the grave tensions between the parties representing the former Northern and Southern states. Their disputes over the new economic and political programs were underscored by previous discord. The deepening rift between the two was revealed when the Yemen Socialist Party of Vice President Ali Salim al-Baydh retreated to his former stronghold in Aden, the former South Yemen capital. This break with President Salih's General People's Congress threw the unified government in Sana into jeopardy at the end of 1993. In early May 1994, a full-scale civil war erupted between the forces of the North under President Salih in Sana and the South under Vice President al-Baydh in Aden, who accused General Salih's forces of killing dozens of his supporters over the past two years and seeking to marginalize the South. As of this writing, the fate of a united Yemen is still in the balance.

Foreign threats can sometimes serve as glue for a reunited state and provide a mechanism for reconciliation. Before Yemen's reunification, Saudi Arabia had looked with misgivings on the Marxism in the PDRY. But once the South dispensed with its communist orientation and the North tolerated political pluralism, the new Yemeni polity stood in sharp contrast to its neighbors' monarchical and autocratic regimes. The melding of the Yemeni military establishments, for example, may have been enhanced by concerns about Saudi Arabian hostility to Yemen's democratic drift.

With the collapse of Moscow's rule in East Europe and the ensuing disintegration of the Soviet Union, a reunified Germany had no external threat to help adhere its divided parts. If history serves as a guide, then a reunified Korea may well face challenges from its powerful neighbors—China, Japan, and Russia. Those challenges can promote Korean nationalism and assist in healing its divisions.

North Korea, East Germany, and South Yemen offer variations on the developmental models of former communist states making the transition from totalitarianism to political pluralism and free markets. Those states in Central Europe as well as the former Soviet Union must transform themselves, aided only by foreign financial and technical assistance. By contrast, the formerly divided states in the new Germany and the new Yemen can count on help from their wealthier halves. Yet those states face a different kind of handicap—integration.

Because those new polities are made up of formerly divided states— separated from their siblings not only by ideology but also by heavily policed borders, suspicion, fear, and envy—the transition to Western economies and politics will be accompanied by political reunification along with a socio-economic sea change.

Leadership and Political Vision

The critical factors of political leadership and vision, when present in constructive ways, can attain extraordinary achievements, as occurred in Western Europe and the United States in the critical period following World War II. At that time, visionary leaders put in place policies that resulted in rebuilding Western Europe, stabilizing East Asia, reconstructing Japan, containing Soviet advances beyond the Elbe River, and reintroducing democracy into West Germany, Italy, France, and other Nazi-occupied lands.

German reunification called for political leadership of a high order by Chancellor Helmut Kohl, whose pivotal role has been eclipsed by the apparent smoothness of the reunification. Kohl's political astuteness was evidenced at a meeting in July 1990 when he negotiated full sovereignty and North Atlantic Treaty Organization membership for Germany with Soviet leader Mikhail Gorbachev, the reluctant British, and the fearful French.[7] Kohl got Moscow to agree to move Soviet troops out of East Germany, no mean achievement, given past Red Army interventions, although it looks easy in hindsight and was not completed until late 1994. Kohl's diplomatic feat during the reunification process has been obscured by persisting East German underdevelopment and united Germany's overall economic slump in the early 1990s.

Difficulties in German unification, as well as Soviet concerns, were overcome by employing the two-plus-four formula, whereby reuniting the two Germanys was placed within the diplomatic framework of the four international powers—Britain, France, the United States, and the Soviet Union. A similar arrangement may be needed in North and South Korea because of the security problems posed by Pyongyang's buildup of nuclear weapons and historical Korea as a point of contention among Japan, China, and Russia. (The United States and Russia could form the other interested parties in an international framework.) Yemen's unification also strengthens the observation that leadership is crucial. Had it not been for President Salih, a soldier of tribal background with little formal education who first moved northern Yemen in a republican direction, there may have been no amicable unification with the People's Democratic Republic of Yemen.

When such far-reaching political leadership and vision are lacking, the outcome is much different. In contemplating the reunification of the Korean peninsula, the case of American reunification after the Civil War is instructive, although the two regions differ greatly in historical, cultural, and political circumstances.

In the case of the American Civil War, the greatest trauma in the history of the United States, the Northern states had been guided by the sure hand of Abraham Lincoln throughout the conflict. During the last weeks of the war and Lincoln's life, he called for clemency toward the South following its all-but-certain defeat. Lincoln's Second Inaugural Address (March 4, 1865), indeed, delineates a postwar policy of reconciliation, healing, and rebuilding. He called for "binding the nation's wounds; to care for him who shall have borne the battle, and for his widow, and his orphan." This was to be done "with malice toward none" and "with charity for all." Had Lincoln lived to finish his second term, American reunification, rather than prolonging and enflaming the wartime divisions between the North and the South, might have taken a far different tone and direction. America's reuniting was accomplished by armed forces and military occupation after the South was compelled to surrender. So far, the German reunification has escaped the pitfalls associated with the reuniting of the American North and South, which to this day gives rise to distinct regional feelings and the near dominance of one political party in the former Confederate states.

Reunification by conquest, however, is not a likely scenario for the Koreas. Most analysts assume a replay of the German model whereby communism in the North collapses or is overthrown by a popular uprising. The two states will then come together peacefully. This scenario does not envision a return to the armed conflict that occurred on the Korean peninsula in the early 1950s. (Yet it should be emphasized that the East Germans and South Yemenis did, in practice, unconditionally surrender their existing socialist system for a free-market economy.)

As happened after the bitter American Civil War, each side in the divided Korea still harbors a great deal of animosity toward its wartime adversary.[8] Overcoming that mutual resentment will take time and political leadership from Seoul if the accepted scenario of the South prevailing over a collapsed communist North is to be realized. To avoid the protracted regionalism and retarded economic development of the American experience after the military defeat of the Southern states, the South Koreans will need to adopt a policy of noble generosity to those north of the thirty-eighth parallel. As Winston Churchill wrote in his pithy epigraph in *The Gathering Storm*: "In victory: magnanimity." Healing the divisions and allaying suspicions will require policies similar to those followed by the United States after World War II toward its defeated German and Japanese foes.

It is in the social, psychological, and symbolic realms that political leadership and vision will be sorely tested by Korean unification. In the case of the American South, Lincoln's death paved the way for the ills of the

Reconstruction period (1867–1877), which lengthened and embittered the reunification on the North American continent. His successor, Andrew Johnson, could not carry out Lincoln's moderate course of action for Southern readmission to the Union. The radical Republicans, who resented a lenient political settlement, resolved on a harsh policy. Instead of mechanisms for reconciliation, some influential Northerners sought punishment and some Southerners wanted revenge for their defeat. In the end, Reconstruction led to sectional bitterness, an intensification of the racial issue, and the development of one-party politics in the South that has only begun to break down.

Again, the reunification of North and South Korea may differ substantially from the German, Yemeni, and American experiences. But unlike Germany and like America and Yemen, the Korean North and South have fought a war against each other, albeit four decades ago. As with most civil war experiences, the bitterness lives on among the former combatants and their descendants. And South Korea, like West Germany, will have to deal not only with economic issues but with the leadership of the Korean Workers' Party and with secret police, informers, and the perpetrators of crimes against average citizens. The revelations in the *Stasi* files of those who collaborated with the fallen regime and spied on their fellow citizens will agitate German society for some time to come and may offer glimpses of how North Korean society will be affected after reunification.

The new government in a reunited Korea will encounter a daunting set of political, social, and psychological difficulties to accompany the much-discussed economic impediments. Like the reunified Germany, it must, for example, settle on the treatment of those who took part in political murders, torture, and spying. The new government must deal with claims of those who lost property, farms, and factories to the communist regime and confront intellectuals, journalists, teachers, military officers, and bureaucrats, along with party officials, who supported the regime for their own gain. It must dismantle and, perhaps, absorb elements of North Korea's military forces. It must handle the psychological sense of betrayal and defeat that will pervade North Korean society. And, foremost, it must reeducate and inspire a society unfamiliar with the workings of free-market economies. These awesome political challenges entail a fundamental readjustment of societal norms, ideals, and personal codes.

Other events of the East and West German unification are instructive. The morning after the collapse of the North Korean regime may see the wholesale flight of Northerners into the Republic of Korea, particularly those who have relatives below the demilitarized zone, as happened in Germany. First, the South Korean leadership will need to decide on an asylum policy for an exodus and to devise methods of implementing that policy. Second, Seoul will require a decision as to when the Northern regime ended. This will be relatively easy if Kim Il Sung or Kim Jong Il are over-thrown by democratic forces who renounce communism and seek reunification. But it will be trickier if the current DPRK regime is replaced by a reformist clique or military government bent on preserving some of the status quo. In South Yemen, the members of the Marxist government needed unification to maintain themselves in power. More important, their Northern opposites were willing to share government posts with them, suggesting that the ideological divisions were not as deep as between the two Germanys or the two Koreas. Postcommunist North Korea will be ripe for civil conflict if factions come into conflict or revanchist elements in the South reclaim properties lost to the communists. In all likelihood North Korea will be in acute need of large-scale and immediate assistance in the form of food, medicine, and medical care.

The German experience also offers insights into social problems after reunification. The postunited Germany is plagued not only by economic dislocations, strikes, and unemployment but by the politics of envy. West German taxpayers, for example, resent giving Easterners aid. Estimates place expenditures on East Germany's socioeconomic recovery at US $100 billion a year for a decade or more after reunification. Thus, the national sacrifice will be long lasting. Furthermore, Western industrialists resent paying West German wages to East German employees whose inferior work habits were formed by a socialist ethos that inspired the memorable phrase "we pretend to work and they pretend to pay us." Worker morale and discipline have been shattered by forty years of mismanagement.

For their part, the East Germans resent their Western counterparts for living well, for trading with countries formerly barred to them, and for enjoying a consumer society. Stripped of its advanced manufacturing base by the Soviets after World War II, East Germany remained shackled to Moscow's increasingly outdated economic system, which led to a stagnant and backward industrial capacity unfit for competition with free-market production. Similar problems in Korea will challenge the ROK leadership to envision policies and programs to lift the North from retrogression and deterioration. Like the American South (whose impoverishment was largely caused by the Civil War), North Korean society will be a long time converging with its powerful sibling state. Seoul will need to arrive at mechanisms for reconciliation that span the different sectors of North Korean society and link them with similar institutions in the South.

In the United States the economic convergence of the rich North and the poor South, in fact, is still going on. The good news is that the South has tended to grow significantly faster in terms of per capita income than the North. Additionally, the South did well after Reconstruction and especially well between the 1940s and the 1970s. The bad news from the American experience is that progress was checked by economic and political events, such as economic shocks affecting southern agriculture or the oil problems of the 1980s or World War II's positive influence on the northern and western regions. The second piece of bad news is that economic convergence between regions is slow, about 2 percent a year in per capita terms for the United States. The result is that economic convergence has taken not decades but generations.[9]

Political and social convergence in America has also taken generations and is far from complete. The Reconstruction period saw embittering cleavages, which, if they surfaced in a postreunified Korea, would bode ill for reconciliation. During Reconstruction, Northern interlopers, or carpetbaggers, moved South, where they gained political control with the aid of federal troops and discriminatory laws. Many Southern whites resented and opposed their intrusion. The regional divisions between the states were also intensified by splits within Southern society itself. The "scalawags" were white Southerners who collaborated with the Republican Party's goals of radically reconstructing the defeated South by enfranchising the freed slaves and by punishing former Confederate leaders. That these scalawags financially gained from their cooperation only increased the animosity toward them by other elements of the post–Civil War society.

In Germany's reunification, West German business interests gained economic control over many of the assets in the East, thereby engendering local resentment. In Russia, the collapse of communism was followed by former Communist Party officials parlaying their power connections to garner wealth and influence in the emerging society. Russia today is characterized by widespread corruption and the formation of a Mafia criminal class, which threatens economic development and undermines the legitimacy of the political process. Any farseeing government must anticipate and seek to ameliorate these types of problems before long-term harm is done to the reconciliation process.

The reunification of North and South Korea may not be as protracted as it has been in America, but it promises to test political leadership as it tries to create and implement visionary solutions to the attendant problems. In the Yemeni case, the border between the two countries was demilitarized, and the two states then permitted their respective citizens to cross freely into each other's territory. Next, they connected electrical grids. These steps developed confidence while building mechanisms for reconciliation between the two societies. Even so, the subsequent political unease between the North and the South and the polarization leading to outright civil war underline the immense difficulty of sustaining the process of reconciliation.

To avoid the American experience of the Reconstruction period as well as the postunification Yemeni experience, South Korean leaders should put reconciliation mechanisms in place in the government, political parties, corporations, trade unions, universities, schools, churches, military, and other institutions that are designed to include Northerners, particularly those untainted by high-level attachments to the power structure in Pyongyang. If announced before reunification, those measures will not only offer inducements for reconciliation but provide a psychological preparation for the South Korean population. Lincoln's objective was to establish a vehicle whereby seceding states could return to the national fold.

The South Korean government could take the lead in such a policy. But its primary goal should be to encourage other elements in South Korean society to adopt reconciliation policies and programs. Reunification is, after all, a societal coming together, not just two governments deciding on political issues.

Notes

1. Tokyo Associated Press dispatch, *Korea Times*, March 23, 1993.

2. *Korea Annual: 1992* (Seoul: Yonhap News Agency, 1993), p.276.

3. Dirk Verheyen, "Dimensions of the German Question," in *Politics of Divided Nations: China, Korea, Germany and Vietnam—Unification, Conflict Resolution and Political Development*, ed. Quansheng Zhao and Robert Sutter, Occasional Papers/Preprints Series in Contemporary Asian Studies, no. 5 (Baltimore: University of Maryland Law School, 1991), pp. 118–21.

4. L. H. Gann, "East Germany: From Partition to Reunification, 1945–1990," in *Politics in Western Europe*, ed. Gerald A. Dorfman and Peter J. Duignan (Stanford: Hoover Institution Press, 1991), pp. 203–7.

5. Robert D. Burrowes, "Prelude to Unification: The Yemen Arab Republic, 1962–1990," *International Journal of Middle East Studies* 23, no. 4 (November 1991):491–92.

6. Robert D. Burrowes, "The Yemen Arab Republic Legacy and Yemeni Unification," *Arab Studies Quarterly* 14, no. 4 (Fall 1992):62–65.

7. For more information, see Renata Fritsch-Bournazel, *Europe and German Unification* (Providence, R.I.: Berg Publishers, 1992), p. 130.

8. Pyo-Wook Han, *The Problem of Korea Unification: A Study of the Unification Policy of the Republic of Korea, 1948–1960* (Seoul: Research Center for Peace and Unification of Korea, 1987), p. 26.

9. Robert Barro, "Eastern Germans' Long Haul," *Wall Street Journal*, May 3, 1991, p. 12.

5

Forging a Common Security View: Prospects for Arms Control in Korea

Man Won Jee

The Realistic Possibilities of Korean Reunification

The unification of Germany through the process of "absorption" was costly in monetary terms and also caused a substantial amount of economic chaos. These results, in turn, remind many Koreans, who have looked forward to the peninsula's reunification, of the problems that unification presents. In addition, Koreans who have incurred private expenses during the visits of immigrant relatives from Yeonbeon, China, have already had, on a microscale, an early taste of the economic burdens of reunification.

Many Koreans in both the South and the North do not look forward to national reunification through absorption. In the South, many are primarily concerned about the economic implications. In contrast, those in the North fear absorption and feel that any form of peaceful reunification is impossible as long as Kim Il Sung or Kim Jong Il maintain political power in Pyongyang. This is because peaceful reunification will cause the opening, or glasnost, of the North, which will then undoubtedly lead to mass hostilities against Kim Il Sung's half-century-old totalitarian repression and the fatal end of Kim Il Sung and his son.

That the South does not desire reunification through absorption suggests that it does not want to see the North's political system disintegrate. South Korea, then, views reform in the North as something that should not be externally forced because the disintegration of the North's political system would lead to a political vacuum followed by social chaos. Such events would, in turn, cause a mass migration of refugees to the South, making reunification through absorption inevitable. Consequently, the most desirable course would be the emergence of a reformist force, other than Kim Jong Il, which can succeed Kim Il Sung even at the cost of taking a similar path to that of the South during the 1960 military revolution.

The South would even prefer the continuation of the North's existing political system under Kim Jong Il as opposed to the possibilities of disintegration, illustrating the predominance of realistic interest over the strong emotional desire for national reunification. The South Korean people wish to see the emergence of reformist forces in the North, first, because they sincerely want the severe repression of their counterparts in the North lifted. Second, there is a strong desire to end the wasteful competition in military and diplomatic areas and to shift these efforts into common national prosperity. Consequently, the probability of how long a regime under Kim Jong Il will survive depends on how soon the worsening economic conditions in the North give rise to reformist forces.

In the past, South Korea has consistently pushed for reform in Pyongyang by requesting reform through direct dialogue as well as appealing to regional Asian powers to use their influence on the North. Although this seems to indicate that the South Korean government has sought the disintegration of the system of the North, the South Korean government has openly stated that it does not seek North Korea's disintegration. This is a contradictory policy. The new administration in Seoul has chosen to accept this illogical policy, first set forth by the Sixth Republic, and continues to maintain the simplistic North Korean policy of the past, which focuses on the reform of Pyongyang, economic assistance, and the nuclear issue.

Kim Il Sung did not naively follow the South's request for reform and his successor likely believes he can maintain his current political system, in which citizens are still required to obtain passes to visit neighboring villages. Thus, the more Seoul pushes for reform, the more he will see this as an attempt to undermine his authority and the more firmly he will close the door to the South. Currently, South Korean items sold in the North are repackaged by Pyongyang to conceal the products' true origin, meaning that all economic transactions between the North and South can only be conducted through covert exchanges. In short, Koreans in the North cannot be allowed to know that their siblings in the South maintain a higher standard of living. After all, North Koreans have been encouraged to believe that one of their responsibilities is to liberate their fellow South Koreans, who are currently living in poverty and hunger.

Two Views

There are two main views on how Seoul should pursue its North Korean policy. The first view asserts that, through economic assistance, Seoul should attempt to shift the basis of Pyongyang's policies from ideology to rational pragmatism, which would improve the quality of South-North dialogue. The second view argues that, by isolating the North on an economic level, Seoul should pursue reunification through either military or economic means. Although the South has tended to follow the first path, the emerging nuclear issue has caused the United States to ask that Seoul consider the second view as well.

The first option, economic assistance, has several problems. First, any attempt to alter the mind-set of those in the North through economic assistance would be more difficult and time-consuming than the half century it took to promote similar changes in the South. Second, continuing economic assistance has indirectly prolonged the military strength of North Korea. As a result, the South will be forced to increase its own military budget correspondingly, resulting in a boomerang effect on the original initiative. Third, the deterioration of the quality in South-North dialogue has not been caused by the lack of rational pragmatism among Pyongyang's leaders; rather, it derives from their belief that glasnost and peaceful reunification are contradictory to their own interests. Similarly the second view, isolation, has profound drawbacks in that is it based on the likelihood of either a system takeover or reunification through absorption.

Unfortunately, Seoul's views toward North Korea have lost most of their meaning because both policies are based on pursuing an "ideal" through nonanalytic means rather than concrete objectives. Previous governments in South Korea have used the emotional issue of reunification to justify policies and control the population rather than evaluating it as a vital national goal. The issue of reunification was first dealt with as a substantive topic by the government beginning in 1980. At that time, the Chun Doo Hwan regime was having problems of legitimacy at home and abroad. As a result, Pyongyang began aggressively discrediting the government in Seoul both internally and externally.

Because articles in the press and even casual discussions on the topic of reunification had been severely restricted by Seoul for thirty years, Pyongyang's proposal for a Democratic Confederal Republic of Koryo caused a commotion in both the international community and the South. Owing to the sudden and rapid spread of support for the Democratic Confederal Republic of Koryo, the Chun regime was forced to put forth its own credible proposal. To do so, Chun extensively expanded the size and activities of the National Reunification Board and numerous other advisory groups on reunification. Nevertheless, from the Chun to the Roh Tae Woo regime, many of these advisory groups have been used primarily to maintain political power.

Issues of reunification and national security are serious concerns for the people of the South. These concerns, however, have been nothing more than the means for the military government to justify the continuation of its rule. Furthermore, although the National Reunification Board and the Advisory Body for Peaceful Reunification are constitutionally recognized organizations, many activists have been detained or arrested for voicing their opinions on reunification. Most South Koreans recognize that, rather than developing the reunification issue into legitimate national security concerns, the military governments of the past have made it a means of domestic control, using it as propaganda to maintain power. South Koreans' desires for reunification have long been repressed under the justification of national security. Nevertheless, because reunification is the most profound and emotional goal of Korean nationalists, the topic becomes more popular the more it is used as propaganda.

Proposals for Unification

Although the Chun Doo Hwan regime operated a large-scale reunification organization, it also kept a safe distance from North Korea because Chun lacked both legitimacy and a clear reunification policy. During his administration, Chun claimed that Pyongyang was constructing a dam on the Kumkang River that would be used to flood Seoul. He then collected approximately a hundred million dollars from South Korean citizens to build a "Peace Dam" to protect Seoul. The reservoir was never filled with sufficient water, however, and the project produced very little aside from weeds and crabgrass. This effort diverted public attention from the actual problems that jeopardized his regime. The two major reunification organizations that he created were almost as wasteful as the "Peace Dam" in that they, too, produced very little aside from propaganda.

The subsequent proposal put forth by the government in the South was the Korea National Community Unification Formula. There are few South Koreans, however, who have been able to grasp the basic concepts behind this proposal. Whereas the Koryo Confederation was a proposal that was easy to understand, the Korea National Community Unification Formula was hardly persuasive even after a long and exhaustive explanation. The South Korean government has yet to put forth another proposal. In short, it has done nothing more than create a large organization without a clear ideology or objective. South Koreans know very little about proposals for reunification. The fact that such proposals are still confusing and highly subject to interpretation illustrates that Seoul has yet to change from its previous role into a new and constructive force.

Because Pyongyang has failed to reunify the nation through military force, the only remaining options are through peaceful means or absorption, either of which will mean the end of the Kim dynasty rule. As a result, Pyongyang's proposals, including the Koryo Confederation, are either propaganda or advocate mutual coexistence and prosperity. Although reunification is unquestionably the most widespread and deepest collective wish of all the Korean people, it has been used as a contest of self-interest between two opposing political systems, justifying both the North's invasion during the Korean War and the years of repressive measures throughout South and North Korea.

In the past, the South has feared Pyongyang's threat of reunification through military force. Now the North fears the threat of absorption by Seoul through glasnost. In the past, Pyongyang attempted to use military force to reunify Korea under socialism; now, however, the South is trying to use its economic and diplomatic power to absorb the North under a nationalist system. Both the South and the North have spent a tremendous amount of money over the past half century in the name of reunification. In essence, both sides have been fighting over whether the resulting government of reunified Korea should be democratic or communist. Unless one side willingly yields, the result will be either reunification under absorption or everlasting hostilities. In some ways, reunification is similar to a shadowy image reflected in water. If both sides continue to grab for it, it becomes even more elusive; if both sides abandon their efforts, it will become easier to make out. This is the paradox of Korean reunification.

Similar to the way in which military hostilities between the two sides were terminated by a cease-fire during the Korean War, both Koreas must now cease trying to reunify. Both sides must coexist without interference— similar to the way in which South Korea's relations with Japan have evolved. Both South Korea and North Korea will be better off if the efforts for reunification are postponed. This would end the costly arms races and hostile diplomatic competition and allow mutually beneficial economic cooperation. Although this might sound like simple common sense, both Seoul and Pyongyang have failed to recognize it.

The path toward the reunification of the Korean peninsula is a long one, and until it is achieved, it is necessary to maintain a peaceful coexistence. During this process, the vast economic, cultural, and ideological gap between the two states will gradually close. In the meantime, both sides must reduce the extensive wastes of confrontation and allow the people of the South and North to pursue an enhanced quality of life. The South Korean government must clarify its reunification policy by stating which of the following policies it intends to pursue: a direct shift from the current confrontation to reunification or a gradual transition from confrontation to peaceful coexistence followed by reunification.

In April 1993, Pyongyang announced a Ten-Point Program for Détente between the South and North Korean People. Points three through seven propose peaceful coexistence (the other five points are brief explanations of the proposals). Up until now, Kim has argued that "liberating the people of the South" is one of the state's most urgent goals. Thus, Kim's only possible justification for such a delay lies within the framework of reunification under a confederation.

There are two main requisites for peaceful coexistence in Korea. The first one is reducing the military, and the second one is eliminating suspicion about the other's military power. As long as mutual distrust exists, the arms race will continue, thwarting the chances of peaceful coexistence. To eliminate such suspicion, there should be a joint control of forces under the active but objective eyes of neighboring states. It would be meaningless to promise peaceful coexistence while preparing the military and maintaining mutual distrust.

For the past half century, both South Korea and North Korea have carried on an arms race based on hatred and mistrust. The Korean War, initiated by the North, resulted in the death of four million people as well as the separation of ten million families. Thereafter, the North continued to send armed infiltration units throughout the South to carry out terrorist activities. As a result, the South Korean population has had much to support its ardent anticommunism. That this attitude has weakened can be attributed to the policies of the military governments in Seoul who chose to use this anticommunism as an excuse for extending their rule and punishing those who showed any opposition. Nevertheless, anticommunism is deeply imbedded among those in the South; the only form of acceptable peaceful reunification remains absorption.

Mistrust toward Pyongyang increased dramatically in 1992 when the North unilaterally abandoned the Agreement on Reconciliation, Nonaggression and Exchanges and Cooperation. Within a year Pyongyang announced its withdrawal from the nuclear Non-Proliferation Treaty (NPT) as well. As a result, the North's promises to maintain a peaceful coexistence carry little weight in the South when accompanied by such overtly mistrustful actions.

Furthermore, a peaceful coexistence can flourish only when both sides no longer feel threatened by each other's military forces, which means that, in addition to the mutual reduction of armed forces, some form of joint arms control must be established.

The joint forces could assume a form similar to that of the North Atlantic Treaty Organization (NATO) forces, in which a unified command structure employs checks and balances throughout the system. This would differ fundamentally from the formula for confederation, whereby a national president is elected by a nationwide ballot to administer joint military control. Such a confederation would be virtually impossible to achieve in the Korean context. Further, any attempt to reunify the peninsula through peaceful negotiations, aside from the possibility of absorption, would be unrealistic in the foreseeable future. The immense difficulties of South-North negotiations can be seen in the numerous problems that occur in the proceedings of Seoul's National Assembly. Even today, the South's National Assembly functions without any standard operating procedures (SOPs). As a result, each individual bill is dealt with through ad hoc negotiations by the ruling and opposition parties. Thus SOPs are negotiated during the proposal of each bill. The subsequent breakdowns in negotiations result in hostile confrontations that lead to either the passing of bills by the majority party or outbreaks of physical violence. When logic is not respected during negotiations, the end result can only be attained by deceit or force.

Although it may be possible for political leaders of the South and North to yield some military power, it is impossible for them to yield political power. Thus, although it is conceivable that such leaders could support a mutual reduction of arms or a joint control of forces, it is improbable that they could provide a unified government through peaceful means. (There are two main reasons any in-depth analysis on the issue of reunification in Korea has been impossible thus far: The first is that the government has monopolized the right to research the topic. The second is widespread acceptance of reunification as a national goal, which has caused theories that recognize the impossibility or improbability of reunification to be rejected. Nevertheless, it is vital that an objective analysis be put forth to assess whether it is more difficult to achieve reunification or peaceful coexistence.)

To postpone reunification and achieve a reduction of arms in Korea would require a fundamental shift in the understanding of both South-North relations, as well as a total alteration of Seoul's North Korea policy. Many accept the concept of reunification but are reluctant to consider the more achievable task of peaceful coexistence and arms reduction, which means that most of the previous basis of reunification has been logically flawed. Revising Seoul's North Korea policy would mean that the National Reunification Board would be terminated and that the focus of South-North negotiations would shift from glasnost and reunification to peaceful coexistence and arms reduction. Peaceful coexistence, arms reduction, and economic cooperation are all that the process can provide, for Pyongyang's "glasnost allergy" will not allow separated families to be united. We will refer to that trade-off as *unification equivalents*.

Approaches to the Nuclear Issue

Ironically, the unrealistic desire for reunification in Korea has been a crippling factor in actualizing prosperity throughout the peninsula. Officials in both South Korea and North Korea have envisioned reunification as their ultimate national goal. Korea's true national goal, however, should be mutual prosperity rather than reunification, which should be one of many objectives that will lead to the peninsula's prosperity. The notion that reunification justifies the sacrifice of human rights or lives is an archaic leftover from the cold war. Another obstacle to attaining common prosperity in Korea is the issue of North Korean nuclear weapons.

The problem of the North's weapons, although an issue between the United States and North Korea, nevertheless must be dealt with as part of the overall package of problems between South and North Korea because it is Pyongyang's single card. The argument that because the South has no nuclear weapons the North should abandon them holds little merit. Both Seoul and Washington need to approach this issue in fundamentally different ways that must be fine-tuned through cooperative measures between the two countries. Up to now, Seoul's policy on North Korean nuclear weapons has been unable to go beyond the policy held by Washington. The influence and dependency on the United States in this matter are primarily due to Seoul's inability to formulate or put forth its own policies.

There are three ways to make North Korea abandon its nuclear weapons: The first would be to apply pressure on the North through force; the second would be a mutual give-and-take process; and the third would be to eliminate Pyongyang's motives for having nuclear weapons. Up to now Washington has used the first two approaches. The United States, however, has less to offer North Korea than South Korea does. The severest pressure Washington is able to apply is economically and diplomatically isolating Pyongyang. (The strategic bombing of nuclear facilities would result in the outbreak of another Korean War, something that both Seoul and the international community would abhor.)

In reality, then, the most dreadful threat to North Korea is economic isolation, which could lead to Pyongyang's assuming a "neither confirm nor deny" position about its nuclear weapons. Furthermore, because Pyongyang cannot sustain itself for long in economic isolation, it could turn against the United States and expand its nuclear program, which would be an extreme threat to the United States. In short, although Washington is capable of putting immense pressure on Pyongyang, such action has the possibility of backfiring, providing ample reason for adventurism by the North.

South Korea must not rely solely on the United States but must develop its own distinct role when dealing with the nuclear issue. South Korea should begin by evaluating why Pyongyang feels it is necessary to have nuclear weapons. The United States has generally been unable to put itself in the shoes of weaker nations and thus has unwittingly provoked Pyongyang's efforts to develop nuclear weapons. Each time the North has initiated a provocative incident, Washington has responded with the threat of nuclear retaliation rather than that of conventional weaponry, which has resulted in the prideful Kim Il Sung becoming highly sensitive about the issue of nuclear weapons. In the mid 1970s, the United States unilaterally decided to withdraw its military forces in Korea, causing then South Korean president Park Chung Hee to pursue Seoul's own nuclear program. The United States thus provoked its *allies* to develop a nuclear arsenal. (Mounting pressure from Washington brought an end to such programs in the South, but research and development continued in the North.) Consequently, considering that South Korea once sought to develop its own nuclear weapons, Seoul is hardly in a position to criticize similar actions now being carried out in the North.

As indicated above, without U.S. intervention it is likely that South Korea would also possess nuclear weapons, and if Pyongyang is to be criticized for desiring to develop its own nuclear weapons, then Washington is to blame for creating this desire. This means that neither the United States nor the United Nations should put the sole blame on Pyongyang. (Aside from the five nuclear powers, several countries, such as Israel and Pakistan, also now have nuclear weapons.) Thus, the issue of North Korean nuclear weapons should be pursued through negotiations rather than pressure and by finding out and analyzing why Pyongyang feels that such weapons are necessary. To resolve problems, both Washington and Seoul must begin by understanding North Korea's position.

North Korea is presently confronted with three main problems: (1) maintaining its current system, (2) dealing with its domestic economic problems, and (3) falling behind in the conventional arms race with the South. Nuclear weapons can prove to be a significant premium in maintaining the North's current system, as Pyongyang will promote its weapons as a source of national pride. The sagging economy can be justified as a necessary sacrifice to pay for nuclear weapons. On one hand, economic sanctions will likely worsen the North's economy. On the other hand, however, North Korea can use the nuclear card to push for more economic cooperation from the West. If Pyongyang does not hold the nuclear card, then it can resolve its economic problems only through international charity rather than international negotiations.

Nuclear Weapons and the North

North Korea has fallen behind in its competition with the South in the area of conventional weapons. The South has spent billions of dollars in defense expenditures over the past several years for 120 F-16s, as well as numerous new submarines, marine patrol aircraft (P-3C), helicopters, and so forth, whereas the North has not been able to purchase a single new fighter plane. In addition, Seoul has been using its economic and diplomatic clout to force Pyongyang toward glasnost, which is seen by the North as an attempt to push for reunification through absorption. In the face of those threats, Pyongyang is attempting to assure its security through an arsenal of chemical, biological, nuclear (CBN), or long-range weaponry. Nuclear weapons have thus become the only available cure for all Pyongyang's problems. If the South continues its all-out efforts to strengthen its military forces, its requesting the North to abandon nuclear weapons would hardly be persuasive. Furthermore, in proportion to its national economy, North Korea has invested a tremendous amount of resources toward its nuclear program, making it difficult to abandon this program without considerable internal opposition.

North Korea's March 12, 1993, announcement that it was withdrawing from the NPT illustrates Pyongyang's predicament. Had Pyongyang accepted nuclear inspections, one of two things would have happened. One, if it was determined that a nuclear arsenal existed in the North, the United States and the United Nations would have been justified in officially punishing Pyongyang. After all, there is a vast difference between a 99 percent certainty and a proven fact.

Or, two, if the inspection determined that North Korea did not have a nuclear arsenal, then Pyongyang would lose its negotiating card. Thus, it is in Pyongyang's interest to maintain the impression that it possesses such weapons even if it does not. This perspective makes North Korea's future direction on the nuclear issue clear. Pyongyang will most likely neither confirm nor deny its nuclear capability. The more sources that suggest that those weapons do exist will only improve Pyongyang's credibility. If North Korea's decision to withdraw from the NPT was based on the above, then Pyongyang's political skills are indeed impressive. North Korea has already assumed the neither confirm nor deny stance and thus has gained a substantial amount of political leverage.

North Korea's nuclear policy toward the South has thus far been influenced by the tremendous psychological effect of these weapons rather than their objective military value. But South Korea must shift its policy toward a more rational level. For the past several years, North Korea has had the ability to nullify all the population of the South through both chemical and long-range conventional weapons, and South Korea's conventional arsenal is virtually defenseless against such a threat. Thus, North Korea has little military reason to develop nuclear weapons to use against the South, especially given the high probability of international retaliation. The addition of nuclear weapons, then, does not actually increase the military threat against the South; to people already dead from chemical weapons, nuclear weapons do not carry much threat.

If it is determined, without doubt, that North Korea possesses nuclear weapons, Washington will have little choice but to rearm the South with U.S. nuclear weapons and to extend the presence of U.S. forces in Korea to protect those weapons. As a result, Pyongyang would lose much ground in arguing for the withdrawal of U.S. troops. The deeper the suspicion over North Korean nuclear arms, the more unlikely a U.S. withdrawal in the South becomes, for as long as there is an imbalance caused by Pyongyang's ardent pursuit of a nuclear program, it has been solely the United States that has prevented Seoul from following a similar path.

The United States is in an ideal position to assume a leading role in both creating a peaceful coexistence and reducing arms on the Korean peninsula. If Washington continues to deal with the nuclear problem as an isolated issue, however, it will be trapped in a one-dimensional tug of war with Pyongyang, which will most likely result in concessions to Pyongyang because the United States cannot justify its demands on the nuclear issue. Under such circumstances, the inappropriate use of force would damage Washington's international leadership. Thus, Washington should abandon its attempts to deal with the nuclear issue through international mechanisms and view the issue as part of the peninsula's internal problems. Because North Korea's motives for developing nuclear weapons grew out of the problems in the Korean peninsula, the solutions for dealing with those weapons can only be found within a Korean context.

North Korea's Economic Situation

The United States and other economic powers are currently implementing dramatic military budget reductions to deal with international economic competition. Similarly, members of the European Community (EC) are also following this trend of military cutbacks. Among such economic powers, military reforms have become a prerequisite for economic reforms. Because South Korea must compete with these economic powers, it too must accept similar military reforms as a precondition of economic reform. Also, without military reductions, the South will be unable to provide economic assistance to the North.

The current severity of North Korea's economic deterioration threatens to destroy the North's system. According to data from the Board of Reunification, North Korea's total trade in 1991 was only 58 percent of the trade in 1990. Furthermore, the total amount of trade in the North during 1991 (approximately $2.72 billion) was only 1.8 percent of the total trade in the South during the same period. Following the demands made by Russia and China in 1992 and 1993 for hard currency in international trade, the amount of trade in the North is likely to diminish further. On the basis of data from the Board of Reunification, North Korea's economic growth rate in 1990 was − 3.7 percent, in 1991 − 5.2 percent, and in 1992 − 5.0 percent. Unless some sort of dramatic reform is carried out by Pyongyang, the North's economy will continue to decline precipitately.

In 1991, North Korea's total imports of crude oil were were only 3.4 percent of those in the South. Of this total, 1.1 million tons were imported from China, 0.98 million from Iran, and 0.44 million from Russia. Owing to both the demand for hard currency and the changed attitude in Beijing and Moscow, Pyongyang will be forced to rely more heavily on economic revenues from its sales of military weapons to Iran and its crude oil supply will be reduced by more than 50 percent in the near future. In addition, although the total amount of food consumption in the North during 1991 was 6.4 million tons, it was only able to produce 4.42 million tons, or 69 percent of the total consumption. Whereas 63 percent of the North's grain imports rely on Canada, China, and Australia, it is projected that the lack of hard currency will also lead to a reduction in those imports. The forecast for food production in the North looks even more dire when considering that, even if it is able to produce more fertilizer, it lacks the ability to transport it throughout the country. In the past, North Koreans have adapted well to a frugal life. To some extent such conditions can be maintained and tolerated as long as there are at least some marginal improvements in the standard of living. Worsening conditions, however, can threaten the existing system of North Korea.

Economic assistance from South Korea can supply some of the urgent economic necessities of the North. Such assistance, however, must be preceded by military reductions from Pyongyang. For North Korea, the military remains the most important factor in upholding its current system. Hence, any order to reduce the military must be accompanied by an acceptable and justifiable explanation, such as including arms reduction and joint military control under the Koryo Confederation. If such a proposal is made, accompanied by an economic embargo, Pyongyang will be forced to accept Seoul's offer or face disintegration.

Unilateral Military Reductions and the
Appropriate Level of Arms in South Korea

A war between South and North Korea will not be solely based on an imbalance of military forces in the peninsula. Pyongyang knows that any attempt to start a war while in diplomatic isolation would lead to its situation being similar to that of Iraq. North Korea has defined the appropriate timing for launching another invasion as the time when the so-called three revolutionary capabilities have matured. These three factors are the internal capabilities of the North, its diplomatic abilities, and adequate support from sources in the South. Presently, North Korea has attained none of these conditions.

Up to now, the U.S. military forces in Korea have served as a deterrent to the outbreak of war on the peninsula, and it is almost inconceivable that war will occur in Korea as long as they remain. Many believe that the U.S. forces will withdraw from Korea in the near future, but this is unlikely because these forces serve a vital role in protecting Washington's interests in Asia as a whole. This means that Washington will probably want to keep its forces in Korea even if the peninsula is reunified. Moreover, Washington currently receives more than $3 billion for defense expenses from South Korea. Neighboring countries in Asia that are concerned with the uncontrolled growth of the military in China and Japan also want the United States to remain in Asia. Nevertheless, how long the U.S. forces remain depends heavily on the mutual friendship between Seoul and Washington. If Washington pushes too hard on either military burden sharing or trade issues, the goodwill between the two countries will certainly be damaged.

The question is "How much is enough?" when dealing with levels of military force in the post–cold war world. The Soviet Union, which has been responsible for the collapse of the cold war system and unilateral arms reductions, defined these levels as being "reasonable sufficiency." This, in turn, implies a "defensive defense" rather than an "offensive defense." Even these military levels, however, are based on the assumption of a potential enemy. Currently, there are no clearly identifiable potential enemies. Even with its military power, the United States is unable to deal with every single emerging international crisis. Most major conflicts around the globe can only be resolved through a collective effort by allied forces. A military force that assumes allied cooperation is a mutually interdependent force.

Although there are no clearly definable potential enemies, an interdependent force must still set standards for the size and structure of its military. When any country creates a military force that can threaten another, it must not be tolerated by the international community, and this will become the guideline for developing military power. To accomplish this, however, each state will need early warning capabilities, the ability to process intelligence, and the basic strategic capabilities to hold off an enemy until allied forces arrive. These will serve as the minimum requirements for formulating military power. In the future, the level of military strength will be based on the national capabilities and scientific level of each state and will stand as a national symbol of prestige. Such prestige symbols will set the standard for the size and nature of one's future military power.

During the cold war era, the great economic powers of the world relied on economic aid or sanctions as a means to resolve international problems. After the cold war, however, rising regional conflicts are being dealt with through peace-keeping forces or multinational troops sent by the United Nations. This multinational use of force has become essential for policing international order, with the form of cooperation provided by each state directly related to the state's prestige. For example, even though Japan assumed the largest financial burden during the gulf war, approximately $13 billion, it was criticized because of its marginal dispatch of force. That Tokyo seeks to dispatch to multinational forces in the future offensive weaponry equivalent to that of Great Britain and France is directly related to the issue of its national prestige. When one sees these developments in relation to the issue of prestige, it is easier to understand the logic behind the changes in the size and form of the Japanese military. Failing to understand the motives behind Tokyo's military increases could ignite an accelerated arms race among the various Asian states.

In the future, the form and size of South Korea's military must follow the trends of advanced states. Up to now, Seoul has basically followed the developments of North Korea's military. When the North increased the number of its armored vehicles, Seoul followed. Similarly, when Pyongyang expanded the number of special forces units, Seoul followed once again. As a result, Pyongyang took the leading role in arms competition, and Seoul merely followed, making quantitative increases without any strategic philosophy, similar to the broad increases made by NATO forces. Until the 1970s a large military was considered to be a strong military. Today, however, in some cases a single soldier can produce the firepower of a thousand soldiers of the past. Weapons were considered an extension of the skills of their users in the past, with techniques similar to those of the martial arts. Today, many combat weapons have already been programmed by scientists before the actual battles; the task of destroying both the enemy and his facilities is often executed by scientists and mathematicians far from the battlefield. Consequently, the physical and mental strength needed to handle weapons of the past hold little relevance for the scientific wars of the present. South Korea currently maintains an extremely large military force. The preservation of such a force through limited defense expenditures can only result in inferior weapons and the use of "human wave" tactics. These are not the traits of a strong military.

The main argument for a change in South Korea's military lies not in the issue of mutual arms reduction between the South and North but in replacing the existing archaic and ineffectual large military force with a smaller, more-scientifically advanced force. Consequently, reducing arms in the South should not be based on a negotiated mutual reduction with the North but on qualitative improvements based mainly on Seoul's economic ability. As long as people view the issue in terms of mutual reduction, the idea that North Korea has not changed will hinder quality improvement in Seoul's military.

The policy of Pyongyang has yet to reflect the seriousness of the current economic warfare. Similarly, Seoul has not yet evaluated which is more important, the military or the economic threat, and has yet to set its priorities in funding these two areas. Despite North Korea's nuclear weapons (or lack thereof), the current probability of war in the Korean peninsula is the lowest it has ever been. Even few soldiers would argue that the North will invade, as long as the United States maintains its global police role in addition to its military forces in Asia. Thus it is important for the South to take the leading role in reducing military forces.

If Seoul dramatically reduces military spending and force size, it will open Pyongyang's eyes to the seriousness of the economic warfare. It will also help Pyongyang realize the ineffectiveness of maintaining a large military and thus encourage a more science-based military. Shifting Pyongyang's focus from military to commercial issues will not only encourage economic reform and glasnost but serve as a stimulus for the growth of democratic movements in North Korea. It can also be an incentive for Pyongyang to abandon nuclear weapons. Furthermore, by reducing its military, South Korea can realize the following benefits: First, the North will abandon its nuclear weapons; second, there will be military reductions in the North; third, a considerable amount of Seoul's defense expenses will be saved; fourth, by shifting more than 300,000 of South Korea's top-quality workforce to the commercial sector, Seoul will gain a total of one trillion won in annual GNP; and fifth, there will be a smaller but more high-tech military.

Arms Reduction and the Creation
of a South-North Joint Command

If peaceful coexistence and common economic prosperity are to exist throughout the Korean peninsula, then both sides must shift the barrels of their guns away from each other. The ideal model for pursuing peaceful coexistence and common economic prosperity is the European Community. It is meaningless for South Korea and North Korea to profess peaceful coexistence while retaining massive military forces near the demilitarized zone. Only by reducing the military can there be a persuasive and credible catalyst for mutual trust. Another factor in building trust would be redistributing forces and creating a cooperative military structure. If both sides sincerely want peaceful coexistence, it will be possible to create structures like NATO, the U.S.-Korea Joint Command, or the allied forces of Germany and France. The South and North can also establish combined forces for humanitarian purposes, such as medical corps and corps of engineers. To make such proposals credible to Pyongyang, offers such as redistributing forces on a provincial basis and including North Korean officers on the staff of South Korean military divisions and regiments should be considered.

Until now, Pyongyang has taken the leading role in advocating mutual arms reductions and, over the past several years, has been using twenty thousand of its troops as part of its commercial workforce. In contrast, the military of the South opposes military cutbacks. South Korea's military has consistently used the threat of the North to argue against reductions, but the true motives of the military have more to do with the potential damage in prestige as well as the threat to the institutional interests of high-ranking officers.

If North Korea insists on holding nuclear weapons, the only way to neutralize this threat is through nuclear weapons. Conventional weapons would simply not be sufficient. Even if the South's conventional military force was one hundred times stronger than that of the North, it would still be no match against nuclear weapons. Consequently, it remains unjustifiable for Seoul to continue to oppose conventional military reductions based on the development of nuclear weapons by North Korea.

To sum up, this chapter has set forth a rationale and plan for removing the nuclear incentive from North Korea and for turning North Korea's focus from the nuclear to the economic and commercial. A first step is for South Korea to propose and pursue not reunification but peaceful coexistence and common economic prosperity through mutual arms reduction. Heretofore, the military in South Korea has resisted military cutbacks not because it will hurt South Korea but because it will hurt the military. However, the proposed military cutbacks would reduce the quantity but improve the quality of the South's conventional military force.

6

Scratching an Old Wound: Japan's Perspective on Korea and Its Unification

Tetsuya Kataoka

A divided Korea belongs to the genus of nations split by the cold war. Because of that split, the two halves represent radically different political systems, each with its own superpower patron. Where unification has succeeded, it was due to armed conquest, as in the case of Vietnam, or absorption of the weaker half by the stronger half, as in the case of Germany. An important precondition for such unifications has been disruptions in the superpower balance. The weakening of one superpower's support for its client caused the client to be conquered or absorbed by the stronger rival.[1]

The German unification was a peaceful absorption made possible by the collapse of the Soviet empire in Eastern Europe. The recent unification fever in Korea is an exclusively South Korean phenomenon that was triggered by the German success and sustained by the collapse of the Soviet Union, which drastically altered the balance of power in Korea's environs. But the fever now appears dashed by the discovery that China is emerging once again as North Korea's friend while U.S. commitment to the Republic of Korea (ROK) is on the wane. That leaves Japan as a friend of South Korea, but rising U.S.-Japan tension will force Japan to contemplate a regionalism comparable to that now under way in Europe and North America. If Japan's American connection falls apart, Japan will most likely seek China's protection within the Asian bloc. If that happens, Korea may be unified on Pyongyang's terms.

But the U.S.-Japan alliance could acquire a new lease on life through a model change that could stabilize the status quo on the Korean peninsula. Under such circumstances Korea's unification will occur only if its neutrality is guaranteed by all the major powers directly concerned, namely, Japan, China, Russia, and the United States. Thus a consensus of six parties (the just-named four and the two Koreas) is needed for unification to be accomplished, a difficult proposition at best. The two-plus-four formula used for German unification was a subterfuge; there were really only two— Chancellor Helmut Kohl and President George Bush. All six parties to the Korean case, in contrast, will insist on pursuing their own national interests. As a general proposition, in unifying a communist and a noncommunist state into one, insisting on peace as a condition may well make it a time-consuming exercise. (This proposition will also certainly apply to the China-Taiwan case.)

The foregoing is based on the concept of a balance of power. Using it as a framework, let me proceed with some observations on international relations surrounding Korea.

Unification fever swept South Korea in the immediate aftermath of the fall of the Berlin Wall and the breathtaking German unification, giving rise to hopes that Korea would be able to reproduce the German feat, that is, through South Korea's absorbing North Korea. This was by no means a pipe dream. The Soviet empire had disintegrated and cast off Pyongyang as an excessive burden. An isolated China was busy fending for itself. For instance, China decided to woo Japan as a buffer between itself and the United States; Beijing's cordial handling of the Japanese emperor's visit in 1992 stunned Japan's Foreign Ministry; and Beijing gave the cold shoulder to its fraternal Pyongyang regime while normalizing relations with Seoul. At the same time the ROK enjoyed the solid and reliable support of the Bush administration, which was not shy about being the world's only superpower. If Bush could apply half the pressure on Pyongyang that he had applied on Baghdad, Kim Il Sung might be convinced of the futility of holding out. But hold out he did. The North Korean leader gained grudging admiration from Southern politicians for having nerves of steel and desperado smarts.

The situation turned for the better for the North, which ultimately must be ascribed to China's emergence as North Korea's sole patron. In the tie that binds Pyongyang to Beijing, ideology counts for less than history and geopolitics; North Korea seems to satisfy China's geopolitical needs for a buffer, as witness Kim Il Sung's fond talk about the concept of a great rear, an obvious reference to China. In this context, whether or not Beijing is kindly disposed to Pyongyang does not matter. The Korean War precedent surely guided Kim Il Sung's strategy, for it was started by Kim Il Sung with Stalin's backing. China opposed it because its priority was getting back Taiwan, the last vestige of the Chinese civil war. Taiwan was under the control of the Nationalists, close allies of the United States; hence China wanted to avoid a conflict that might jeopardize its retaking Taiwan. But no matter. When the U.S. Army crossed the thirty-eighth parallel on its march to the Yalu River, China had to intervene on Pyongyang's behalf.

Kim Il Sung's talk of the great rear reminds us that Saddam Hussein was defeated in the gulf war because he lost the great rear when Mikhail Gorbachev's Soviet Union chose to cooperate with President Bush. Kim seems to feel, correctly in my view, that the historical and geopolitical ties that bind China to Korea are stronger and more enduring than those that bound the Iraqis to the Russians. The China-Korea connection—resting on geopolitics rather than communist ideology—is being resuscitated by Kim Il Sung.

In preparation for his departure from this world, Kim Il Sung's highest goal was to create a stable and benign international environment for his son and the regime he will head. Because Kim could not hope to unify Korea, his sole purpose was to defend the status quo. North Korea managed to get a seat in the United Nations, parallel with South Korea. But when North Korea attempted to win cross recognition from the United States and was rebuffed, it tried to split Japan off from the United States, a strategy China tried with success when it won Japan's diplomatic recognition following Richard Nixon's trip to China. Kim almost managed to bamboozle Shin Kanemaru, the leader of Japan's Liberal Democratic Party who has since gone down in a corruption scandal. But that was undone by George Bush, who held to the hard line. Bush's primary interest was to keep Korea—both North and South—nuclear free; in view of his close ties to the Beijing leadership, his enthusiasm for Korean unification could be doubted. With Washington's support, the Seoul government carried out brilliant "Ostpolitics," normalizing relations with Moscow and Beijing, thereby outflanking and isolating Pyongyang. The unification fever in South Korea was based on this achievement.

Kim Il Sung laid low and bided his time, hoping for a change in Washington. Undoubtedly, he took heart from the fact that the U.S. victory in the gulf war had rapidly lost its strategic significance. With Saddam Hussein alive and well, the Bush administration was in the end reduced to harassing air sorties. When Bill Clinton came to power, Pyongyang presumably carefully scrutinized his policy and inclinations. Among other things, Clinton's musings about the possibility of talking to Saddam Hussein must have given a strong indication, in Pyongyang's judgment, that the United States was less willing to resort to arms to settle a conflict.

I predicted that Clinton, if elected, would be reluctant to get involved in an infantry war.[2] Yet my study of the Joint Chiefs of Staff's new military doctrine, as gleaned from the gulf war experience, concludes as follows: (1)

that doctrine placed a premium on wars of quick decision and high mobility and abhorred military occupation; (2) it called for a massive and protracted buildup and an overwhelming initial strike; (3) it was extremely costly in fiscal terms; and (4) far from eradicating the so-called Vietnam syndrome, it reaffirmed the aversion to battlefield casualties. Thus the ability to engage in infantry combat is the major condition for concluding a war successfully.

Visible to any observer of U.S. foreign policy, the above points were undoubtedly also taken into account by Pyongyang before it concluded that Bill Clinton, being averse to wars, could be forced to talk if Pyongyang created a mild confrontation with Washington. Pyongyang walked out on the nuclear Non-Proliferation Treaty (NPT) in March 1993; that is, it observed the Clinton administration for three months before implementing its démarche. The walkout on the NPT was a unilateral change in the status quo in Korea and threatening to the United States, which is responsible for South Korea's security. The departure threatened the status quo because it implied that North Korea would be free to proceed with the production of a nuclear arsenal, but Pyongyang did not say whether it was going to do so or whether it was already in possession of nuclear weapons. By merely departing from the NPT, it posed a mild and ambiguous threat that, moreover, was reversible: it could return to the NPT regime.

If the stakes in the confrontation are too high, Clinton might be forced into taking a hard line. Lest the United States be tempted to intervene militarily, Pyongyang announced its readiness to resort to a reprisal by invading South Korea, which would then touch off a second Korean War. By posing an ambiguous and reversible threat, on the one hand, and by sealing off military intervention, on the other, Kim Il Sung succeeded in drawing the Clinton administration into a parley it could not have hoped for from the Bush administration.

But North Korea's initiative was also directed at Beijing, which had been delivering one humiliating blow after another to Pyongyang, the most cutting of which was China's recognition of Seoul in 1992. China did so, I presume, despite Kim's plea that Beijing persuade Washington to recognize Pyongyang in exchange for China's recognizing Seoul. In my view, China was mistaken to ignore North Korea's plea; perhaps it stood to gain something from doing so, a gain that remains concealed from our view. But China must have as much at stake as the United States in avoiding a war in Korea. And it is certainly averse to Korea's unification on Seoul's terms.

Everything was reversed with Kim Il Sung's brilliant single stroke. Clinton, fearing both nuclear proliferation and another war in Korea, agreed to talks. The specter of war also forced China, almost in spite of itself, to be North Korea's great rear once again. Clinton had already recognized Serbia as in Russia's sphere of influence in the Balkans, untouchable by the West.

North Korea now acquired a parallel status, recognized by both Washington and Beijing.

Kim Il Sung's coup put an end to the rumor of unification on Seoul's terms; indeed it put an end to talk of unification. If the United States is willing to talk to avoid a war, it is well on its way to recognizing the government of North Korea. That also paves the way to Japan's recognition, which was another of Kim Il Sung's objectives. He is probably going to get it in exchange for returning to the NPT regime on condition that inspections be bilateral, not unilateral. Bilateral inspection will probably leave a loophole through which Pyongyang can squeak a bomb or two in the future.

But North Korea will not play the bomb card anytime soon, for time is on its side. From here on, it will show its reasonable side. Sooner or later Bill Clinton will be pressured to withdraw the U.S. forces from Korea and even to scuttle the alliance with the ROK. How that pressure will work itself out is unforeseeable at the moment. But there is no doubt whatever that the pressure will increase because Clinton's America is not willing to fight to keep Korea nuclear free and is prepared to connive with a North Korea that is in secret possession of a few bombs.

The position of the U.S. forces in South Korea then becomes awkward, if not untenable. Because American nuclear weapons have been withdrawn from South Korea by President Bush, the U.S. forces in Korea are defenseless unless they can count on Japan's consent to become the platform for retaliatory strikes. But whether Japan will consent to such an arrangement is uncertain. Hence, the U.S. forces are less a trip wire than a provocation, best withdrawn altogether. In any case, Clinton may have in mind conferring the honor of recognition on Pyongyang in order to tame it.

Japan's reaction presumably weighs heavily on Clinton as he charts that course. Today's Japan, however, as indicated by Shin Kanemaru's deal with Kim Il Sung, is agreeable to recognizing North Korea, taking its words of nuclear innocence at face value. If the United States and Japan recognize the North Korean regime, the U.S. forces will be withdrawn from Korea. But, paradoxically, Korea's division will again become stable. Japan's money will begin pouring into North Korea, paving the way for monies from the other parts of Asia, which are affluent these days. North Korea will begin to mimic communist China's capitalist success. We must remember that wages in the North are much lower than in the South. A stable equilibrium will emerge between China, standing behind Pyongyang with Japan, and the United States, standing behind Seoul.

The Korean peninsula, by virtue of its history and geography, is so tightly bound up with Japan's security as to be almost an extension of Japan, in the Japanese perception. In modern times, all the wars in East Asia in which Japan has been involved in also involved Korea. Japan went to war against the Ch'ing empire in 1894–1895 over Korea. When imperial Russia refused to recognize Japan's newly acquired interest, Japan went to war against Russia. Japan went to war against the United States because it demanded that Japan abandon Manchuria—contiguous to Korea—in an ultimatum called the Hull Note.

The American people are inclined to think that those were Japanese warlords' military adventures, provoked by the Japanese themselves. But when the Americans assumed Japan's security responsibilities, they discovered that, geopolitically, Japan cannot be defended unless Korea is secure. So the Americans went to war in Korea in 1950 as Japan's surrogate.

During a lecture at the University of Chicago in 1951, George F. Kennan said the following about that war:

> It is an ironic fact that today our past objectives in Asia are ostensibly in large measure achieved. The Western powers have lost the last of their special positions in China. The Japanese are finally out of China proper and out of Manchuria and Korea as well. The effects of their expulsion from those areas have been precisely what wise and realistic people warned us all along they would be. Today we have fallen heir to the problems and responsibilities the Japanese had faced and borne in the Korean-Manchurian area for nearly half a century, and there is a certain perverse justice in the pain we are suffering from a burden which, when it was borne by others, we held in such low esteem. What is saddest of all is that the relationship between past and present seems to be visible to so few people. For if we are not to learn from our own mistakes, where shall we learn at all?[3]

Some may be puzzled by the statement that Korea is an extension of Japan in the Japanese perception, for the people of Japan have been pointedly ignoring Korea and its people longer than most people can remember. Let me explain why because that will also fortify my contention that Korea is important to Japan.

The man who laid down Japan's postwar foreign and defense policy was Prime Minister Shigeru Yoshida, an ardent imperialist and royalist who was called the Japanese Winston Churchill. The question is, Why should such a man lay down a foreign policy honoring the no-war constitution and abstention from military entanglements, a policy still observed by Japan today? My answer is as follows. Yoshida and his contemporaries spent their lifetimes building the empire in Korea and Manchuria in an attempt to ward off Russian and later Soviet influence. From 1937 on, they also actively fought the Chinese communist forces in north and central China. But Franklin Roosevelt's America was generously disposed toward Stalin and chose to regard Japan as the aggressor. The Pacific war came, and Japan lost everything, including Korea.

Since then the United States has had to fight two wars in Asia, in Korea and Vietnam, that are directly traceable to the destruction of the regional order that Japan had built, although, as Kennan points out, the American people do not seem to be aware of the cause and effect. But Yoshida was keenly mindful of the revolution unfolding in China and Korea in the late 1940s. If he had forebodings of trouble, he was right: less than five years after the United States had driven Japan out of Korea, imposed the no-war constitution on Japan, and disarmed it, a war broke out on the Korean peninsula. And a conflict with the United States was developing in Indochina. John Foster Dulles came to Tokyo to negotiate peace and defense treaties with Japan, the operational purpose of which, though nowhere stated, was to enable the United States to prosecute the war in Korea.

Dulles knew that Japan and Korea were inseparable, which was fine for Yoshida. But Dulles wanted Japan not only to rearm but to join a regional collective security arrangement. That is, he wanted Japan to send troops to Korea. In the 1950s there was a saying that enjoyed wide currency in America, especially among Republicans: "We fought the wrong enemy," meaning we should have fought the Chinese Communists. (Being a Republican, Dulles undoubtedly shared that sentiment.) But it was absurd to the Japanese, and especially to the imperialist Yoshida, to have been kicked out of Korea, disarmed, then told that the Americans had "fought the wrong enemy," and asked to go back into Korea to engage the same Chinese communist forces Japan had engaged before. Yoshida could not stomach the idea of sending his countrymen on such a mission, and so he said no to Dulles, using the constitution as a pretext.

Kennan would have understood Yoshida well. But in 1951 the American people did not understand that America's China venture—carried out in the name of "open door"—had produced a communist monster or that there was a perverse justice in America fighting in Korea. In the full tide of Pax Americana, the United States felt only glory and has remained in Korea for more than forty years, preferring to take full charge of military matters and relegating the Japanese to a minuscule role. But suddenly, in the transition from the Bush administration to the Clinton administration, the mood changed. Now Americans fully understand Kennan's message, which brings us to a major problem.

The Americans have always felt that they liberated the Korean people from the yoke of Japanese colonialism and that, because they had a hand in founding the ROK regime, they encouraged its anticolonial sentiment. At the same time, they created the antimilitarist regime in Japan, a regime that ignored Korea. The chasm between the two nations was bridged by the overarching presence of the United States. Until the end of the Bush administration, Washington had always favored the hub-and-spoke arrangement that put America at the center of a dozen or so bilateral arrangements in Asia. There were no regional or multilateral arrangements, in defense or trade, to tie the Asian nations laterally. Washington preferred bilateral arrangements because it could dominate them.

Worse yet, there has been a recent tendency for Washington to encourage the Korean-Japanese hostility. This tendency surfaced especially at the office of the United States trade representative (USTR) during the Bush administration, which presided over the most intense phase of U.S.-Japan trade friction so far. To young officials of the USTR, Japan is the enemy in a trade war with the United States. Clyde Prestowitz Jr. says that America is "trading places" with Japan. Lester Thurow of the Massachusetts Institute of Technology says that America is in a "head to head" competition with Japan. To win the war, the USTR has been hatching and broadcasting diabolic schemes involving South Korea. According to one, the United States would enlist the ROK in the North American Free Trade Area in order to split the emerging yen bloc headed by Japan. There are many others, some of which have unnerved the officials in Japan's Ministry of International Trade and Industry.

The logic behind the USTR's conduct is by now familiar to those who have been watching Washington. According to that logic, Japan is alien to Western values and totally different from the rest of the free-trading world; hence it must be cast off and ostracized. A spokesman for this point of view, Chalmers Johnson of the University of California at San Diego, says,

> I do believe there should be a change in the American military position in the area [East Asia]. This would include a withdrawal of American ground forces from South Korea, where they are no longer needed. Korea is today the most democratic country in East Asia, certainly more so than Japan. I believe we do want to continue to project power. Surface-navy-type power. We should aim to complicate the decision making of the two big nations— Japan and China. . . . The Clinton policy, if it's an effective one, should be one of explicit balance of power.[4]

Unfortunately, the anti-Japanese sentiment was contagious in Seoul and by now has had a self-fulfilling effect in Tokyo as well. The relationship between the ROK and Japan has deteriorated since the fall of the Berlin Wall, paralleling the rising ethnic tensions elsewhere in the world. Today, the biggest bilateral pending issue is the question of the so-called Korean comfort women, who were forced to serve as prostitutes to Japanese soldiers during World War II. America, then, is still inclined to play up bilateral tension.

But I feel that we are fiddling while Rome burns. America is retreating from East Asia, alarming every country except perhaps China. The United States has already conceded the special relationship between Beijing and Pyongyang. Washington will probably be satisfied if Pyongyang returns to the NPT, even if Pyongyang's nuclear facilities are not thoroughly inspected, because it wants to pull out of South Korea. In early 1994 Clinton and his USTR, Mickey Kantor, collided with Japan over managed trade they want to impose on Tokyo, even though Tokyo has taken a last-ditch stand against it. Although I suspect Clinton is bluffing, he may not be able to go on playing politics for long. If he does collide with Japan, then what? China is on an upswing and will soon surpass Japan in GNP; it has just decided to build, rather than purchase, two aircraft carriers.[5]

Is this a time for Americans to be sowing a rift between Korea and Japan? Is this a time for the Koreans and Japanese to be quarreling with each other? The hostility between the two peoples was preserved as a by-product of the cold war hub-and-spokes structure and predicated on Pax Americana, which is fading. Should Japan's colonialism in Korea, which began nearly a hundred years ago and ended nearly half a century ago, be the central agenda today? Should the Korean people be chiming in with Japan's Socialists and assailing Japanese militarism? Shin Kanemaru's trying to bribe the elder Kim into submission deserved to be lampooned but only because there was a George Bush in Washington who made it irrelevant. But if Washington's new leadership is inclined to sympathize with the Kanemaru thesis, it bodes ill for Asia.

My concern is what appears to be the Clinton administration's assumption that Korea is separable from Japan (the Dean Acheson assumption). The Korean counterpart of that is the assumption that Korea does not need Japan (because it has the United States); the Japanese counterpart is the assumption that Korea can be ignored (because it has stuck Korea on America's back). Can we—the American, Japanese, and Korean peoples—afford to let the U.S. forces in South Korea be withdrawn and sent home? Can those forces be reintroduced in an emergency? Beijing may relish that withdrawal because it could have more influence on the Korean peninsula. If it becomes impossible to reintroduce the U.S. forces to Korea, the ROK-U.S. defense pact may go into desuetude, while China looms over Korea.

Let us suppose that the Acheson doctrine becomes the de facto U.S. policy after the withdrawal of the U.S. forces from Korea. This will nullify the U.S.-Japan defense pact because the original purpose of that pact was to defend Korea. For Japan to learn that the United States will defend Japan but not Korea could have a profound effect on Japanese confidence. The real catastrophe is likely to creep up, unseen and silent, on the Korean peninsula, as always. As a result of the United States pulling out of South

Korea, in several years both the U.S.-ROK and U.S.-Japan defense pacts may be dead.

If Japan then revives militarism, Tokyo may be able to balance China's increased military power. But we may not be so lucky. *The Economist* of London speculated in the first issue of 1993 that a Finlandization of Japan is, as of 1994, a more honest and realistic projection than the militarist scenario. Remember that Japan's former prime minister, Kiichi Miyazawa, believed in the no-war constitution and was even willing to soft-pedal the political reform for fear that it would lead to a constitutional revision and an end to the no-war provision. If Japan becomes Finlandized, the ROK will be isolated. Beijing will help Pyongyang unify Korea on its terms. We will then be on the way to the Greater East Asia Co-Prosperity Zone under Chinese hegemony.

Notes

1. Let me state at the outset that, as a Japanese citizen, I deeply sympathize with the plight of the Korean people for having been divided by the cold war and that I fully support their desire to be reunited. I say this because Japan came close to being divided along the line separating Hokkaido from Honshu and is still divided along the line separating Hokkaido from the Northern Territories. At the same time, I find it difficult to counsel the use of violence as a means to unification. As soon as peace is made an important condition of unification, however, it becomes remote and difficult to attain, calling for patience and perseverance.

2. "Senso o suteta Amerika" ("America abandons wars"), *Voice*, November 1992, pp. 116–36.

3. George F. Kennan, *American Diplomacy, 1900–1950* (Chicago: University of Chicago Press, 1951), p. 52.

4. *Asian Wall Street Journal*, January 20, 1993, p. 4.

5. *Sankei Shimbun*, May 13, 1993, p. 1.

7

Korea's Reunification: Implications for the U.S.-ROK Alliance

Edward A. Olsen

Two key issues facing South Korea in the 1990s are the nature of a prospective unified Korea and the long-term fate of Seoul's military ties with Washington. As of the early 1990s, there is great uncertainty about whether Korea will actually reunify—to say nothing of what it will be like after the event. In contrast, there is considerable confidence that the U.S.–Republic of Korea (ROK) alliance is strong and durable for the foreseeable future. The pros and cons of Korea's continued division or reunification are broader topics than can be addressed here and have been analyzed by many scholars.[1] For present purposes, this chapter assumes that unification will occur. Moreover, it assumes that a unified Korean nation, administered from Seoul, will constitute an enlarged version of the ROK, achieved either through a negotiated reunion or through the collapse of North Korea into South Korea's embrace. Were the unification of Korea to produce control by Pyongyang (presumably through conquest of South Korea), the U.S.-ROK alliance would obviously not continue into the postunification period. Therefore, this analysis focuses on the impact the issue of Korean unification has had, and may have, on the U.S.-ROK alliance.

To date, American and South Korean officials have assumed that there will be a role for U.S. forces in Korea after unification.[2] That assumption may prove to be warranted, but a number of possible circumstances in Korea, in the United States, and in Asian regional affairs could derail such assumptions. All these factors provide the evolving context against which the validity of a U.S.-Korean security alliance will need to be measured. Given the inherent uncertainties attached to the scenarios for Korean unification, mixed with a range of options open to both prospective security partners, there can be little doubt that the unification of the divided Korean nation will influence profoundly the basis on which the current U.S.-ROK security alliance is judged to be "strong" and "durable."

The Alliance since the 1940s

To evaluate the prospects for the future impact of Korea's unification on the Korean-American alliance, it is worthwhile to assess the ways that Korea's division has shaped the alliance since the 1940s and the ways in which that alliance depends on Korea's rupture. Unlike so many of the United States' cold war–vintage alliances, the U.S.–South Korean military bond predates the cold war's formal emergence. The cold war was a way to characterize a series of conflicting events between the United States and the Soviet Union and their perceived proxies, one of which developed in Korea in 1945–1946. Despite the widespread identification of the U.S.-ROK alliance with the cold war, it is more accurately seen as a product of Korea's division. This causal relationship could have immense bearing on the eventual linkages between a reunited Korea and its security ties to the United States.

Once Korea was divided, the United States bore a certain responsibility for its geopolitical protégé. Although easily forgotten after decades of close U.S.-ROK security ties, it is important to recall the caution with which the United States accepted its original responsibility. The American role in Korea initially was almost accidental, an unintended by-product of defeating Japan. Had the Soviet Union's role in accepting Japan's defeat not included a presence in Korea that echoed its more troubling role in Central Europe, the United States might well have rid itself of any substantial security role in Korea. The parallels were there, of course, drawing the United States into a more prominent role in post–World War II Korean affairs than Americans had anticipated. Even that unfolding of cold war repercussions, and the creation of the ROK under United Nation/U.S. auspices, was not sufficient to commit the United States to a major military role in Korea. As indicated by the withdrawal of most U.S. military occupation forces in the late 1940s, the renowned geopolitical disclaimer by Secretary of State Dean Acheson regarding U.S. interests in the Asia-Pacific region, and the coolness of many American officials toward President Syngman Rhee's appeals for U.S. support, Washington was—at best—ambiguous toward South Korea before North Korea's attack.

The reasons behind the American shift to support the ROK against external aggression are complex. The United States was engaged in a larger struggle to enforce containment in the emerging global cold war. Korea was a test case of sorts, a line drawn in the sand, perhaps, to test U.S. resolve. Although the previously tepid U.S. enthusiasm for South Korea's cause could have permitted Americans to abstain from the Korean War, the sneak attack emanating from a communist state probably acting on orders from the Kremlin gave the United States enough reason to shift its position and rescue the underdog. This was sufficient to rally support for an unwanted war from the American people and the U.S. Congress, among whom there remained sizable anxiety about assuming a superpower's leadership role in defending far-flung areas of the world. Because the flush of victory from World War II remained strong, however, even people who wanted to enjoy the fruits of peace did not view this sudden conflict as a major war that would seriously test the United States' capabilities. It was assumed that, once engaged, the United States would prevail. No one at that point entertained the prospect of what would later become known as limited war, with its attendant frustrations. Korea yielded that phenomenon, but Americans did not know it going into that conflict. Thus the shift in U.S. policy toward Korea was achieved quickly and with relatively little opposition.

Much less visible to the American people at the time was another major factor—arguably *the* major factor—motivating U.S. leaders. As Secretary Acheson's statement indicated, the United States' vital regional interests in the emerging cold war were focused on offshore Asia, centering on Japan as the anchor for a fledgling, maritime-based containment effort around the rimland of Eurasia. The attack in Korea underscored what American leaders understood but had not accented lest they play into President Rhee's hands— namely, that the status of Korea mattered to Asian stability. Had North Korea absorbed South Korea slowly via political means, the United States may well have gradually acquiesced. A peacefully communized Korea, not guided by Moscow, probably could have been tolerated by the American government at that point. The violent North Korean attack, however, threatened to spread unrest to Japan and clearly jeopardize America's Pacific stake there, which gave rise to the U.S.-Japan security treaty. Operationally, that treaty permitted Japan to be used as a rear area for waging war in Korea. More important in the long run, the U.S.-Japan military relationship was spurred by American desires to enmesh Japan into the burgeoning Western alliance network to contain Soviet aggression, which was assumed to be behind North Korea's attack on South Korea. This Japan-centered rationale could not be readily stressed so soon after World War II as a reason for Americans to rescue South Koreans from communist assault, but it was very real in terms of U.S. national interests. What the United States might be prepared to do on behalf of its national interests in eastern Eurasia would send signals of the utmost importance to the coalescing rival alliance on the other end of the continent gripped by the fledgling cold war.

Against the background of these developments one can note the diverse dimensions of this formative phase in the U.S.-ROK alliance. Within a matter of days in mid 1950, the alliance developed teeth it had not had previously, Korea became a key theater of the cold war, and Korea's regional context was underlined. The Korean War, precipitated by one Korean state's effort to unify the nation via armed force, thereby infused a level of vitality into the U.S.-ROK alliance it had previously lacked. This amounted to a second phase in the birth of the alliance. More important, the context of the truce that halted the fighting (vice ending the war) three long years later obligated the United States to the indefinite defense of South Korea through deterrence against North Korea. The post–Korean War sense of a quasi-permanent division of Korea along a heavily armed border transformed the U.S.-ROK security relationship into a qualitatively different alliance. Virtually alone in Asia, the inter-Korean border became a parallel to the North Atlantic Treaty Organization (NATO)–Warsaw Pact frontline. Nothing like it existed in other U.S.-Asian alliances, such as those with Japan, Thailand, the Philippines, or formerly with the Republic of China. Only South Vietnam's case resembled South Korea's, but its border was too porous for the parallel with NATO to exist. Aside from the narrowly military significance of that comparison, which made the U.S.-ROK alliance more akin to NATO than were other Asian-U.S. alliances, it is important to note the role the divided Korean state implied for the U.S.-ROK alliance during the decades-long era of deterrence.

The United States' purpose in Korea possessed a contradictory quality. American forces were stationed in Korea to preserve South Korea's freedom and deter North Korea from renewing the conflict. This was a high-minded purpose, but it simultaneously undermined another crucial aspiration of South (and North) Koreans—unification. Washington has consistently dealt with this dilemma by supporting Seoul's stance on the unification issue. In other words, the United States' help in defending South Korea would bolster the ROK in its unification negotiations with the Democratic People's Republic of Korea (DPRK) and not impede the long-term goal of those sporadic talks. Nevertheless, the strength of the U.S. security commitment and the ways it helped South Korea carve out a separate quasi-nation-state identity did have the effect of making the division of Korea a semipermanent fixture of the cold war years. Despite the criticism this situation generated from North Koreans (which could be easily dismisssed) and from South Koreans, who resented the ways in which U.S. forces in Korea tended to prolong Korea's division (not so easily dismissed), there was no way to avoid this reality. Just as Korea's troubled division was a fundamental element in the two-phased birth of the U.S.-ROK alliance, so too was the inherent contradiction (between the extended deterrence function of U.S. forces in Korea and their role in blocking reunification) a fundamental factor in shaping the nature of the alliance.

The cold war years greatly influenced both the issue of Korea's unification and the development of the U.S.-ROK alliance. In turn, the cold war context shaped the ways these two elements in Korean affairs interacted with each other. The cold war's global tensions between the United States and the Soviet Union added another layer of intensity to Korea's division. The U.S.-ROK geopolitical relationship during the cold war intensified South Korea's reasons for hewing to an anticommunist line. Seoul was rewarded by America for adopting a hard-line ideological posture. The ROK thus became a client state whose domestic political excesses would be largely overlooked for a generation by American officials in exchange for ideological fealty. South Korea also became a beneficiary of U.S. efforts to build a network of alliance partners as a bulwark against global communism. This role injected aid, investment, and technology into South Korea in the civilian and military sectors. Seoul also became part of the diplomatic and economic network embodied in the generic Western alliance. This opened many doors for South Korea. It also transformed the ROK societally and geopolitically. The net effect of these developments was to widen the gap between South and North Korea, deepening the division and adding to the already formidable problem of unification.

Cumulatively, the success that South Korea enjoyed as a cold war protégé of the United States effectively changed the value of the ROK to the United States militarily. Before, during, and for a few years after the Korean War, South Korea was far more of a liability than an asset for the United States. As the ROK prospered under U.S. auspices and became a member of a wider U.S.-led security community—pointedly encompassing Japan—its value as an ally grew. Seoul's ability to help the United States wage the Vietnam War—albeit subsidized by Americans—was a step in this direction. Further South Korean economic successes in the 1970s and 1980s fostered a new level of American appreciation for South Korea. The tendency to see the ROK through strategic lenses "made in Japan" was mitigated, though never eliminated. South Korea's intrinsic importance was increasingly recognized as being on a par with its regional significance. This shift had an enormous impact on how Americans perceived and treated South Korea. It emerged from its status as a war-torn, impoverished society—epitomized by its prolonged *MASH* imagery—and assumed a new role as an economic partner and competitor. Strategically, this shift elevated South Korea from a client state to a junior partner in regional security affairs. As positive as many of these developments were for U.S.–South Korean relations, their cold war context stamped them with an identity that aggravated the basic problem of a divided Korea. The closer the United States and the ROK grew, the more alienated they became from North Korea.

This situation was complicated by North Korea's erratic relations with Beijing and Moscow. Although beyond the scope of this chapter, Pyongyang's fence-sitting and tilting toward one or the other of its backers tended to widen the gap between the two Koreas. In short, the Korean peninsula theater of the cold war assumed proportions that gave it a momentum of its own. That dynamic was made still more complex by the ways the two sides in Korea and their superpower cold war backers related to neighboring Japan's position in regional security. That, too, is too large a topic for this chapter to encompass in detail. Suffice it to say that China, the Soviet Union, and North Korea distrusted Japan for separate but overlapping reasons. Those relationships intensified the communist states' suspicions of the U.S.-ROK alliance. It became, variously, a tool of U.S. or Japanese "imperialism" or a plot by both. These perceptions were distinctly different from reality, which points to one of the problems confronted by the U.S.-ROK alliance, especially as South Korea prospered. As noted, Americans had a long-standing tendency to treat Korea as a corollary factor in a more important set of problems confronting the United States and Japan regionally in the cold war. As the ROK grew into an ally and trading partner to be reckoned with, the U.S.-Japan backdrop had to be modified. Tokyo increasingly confronted Americans who ascribed intrinsic value to South Korea. In turn, South Koreans appealed to U.S. willingness to elevate the ROK to a level closer to that of Japan. Aside from dealing with the animosities stemming from Japan-Korea historical frictions, this adjustment process was made more difficult by the differences between the U.S.-ROK and the U.S.-Japan alliances.

The U.S.-ROK alliance was characterized by its focus on the North Korean adversary—not on the key cold war Soviet adversary. In contrast, the U.S.-Japan alliance, although fuzzy about what country to the north was Japan's hypothetical adversary, left no serious doubt that the alliance was part of the core Western system aimed at the Soviet Union. Aside from some naïfs in Japan, few had any illusions about the strategic purpose of the U.S.-Japan alliance in its mature form from the 1960s to the 1990s. Thus, the strategic objectives of the two U.S. alliances with the Northeast Asian neighbors were distinctly different. One (U.S.-ROK) was solely and narrowly regional, whereas the other (U.S.-Japan) was global in nature but only expressed regionally. As both South Korea and the cold war matured, it became increasingly difficult to blur these distinctions. This, in turn, influenced the U.S.-ROK alliance during the Reagan years, when U.S. policy in Northeast Asia became increasingly aimed at the "evil empire." The notion that the United States was in Korea largely to cope with North Korea's threat became less persuasive as the years passed, as the Soviet offshore threat increased in the 1980s, and as South Korea became (like Japan) more capable of being a strategic partner with whom U.S. burdens should be shared.

Had the global cold war not ended when and how it did, there arguably could have been either a thorough merger of the ROK into a larger U.S.-led collective security system not aimed at North Korea or a significant parting of the ways as Seoul and Washington pursued different objectives versus different adversaries. Neither occurred, largely because the cold war ended. That event has reshaped world affairs and is certain to influence Korea for some time.

The end of the global cold war influenced Korea in ways that are subject to varying interpretations. All of them bear on the interrelated issues being addressed here: Korean unification and the U.S.-ROK alliance. On the surface it appears that Korea was largely a bystander to the events in U.S.-USSR and European affairs that are characterized as the end of the cold war. Certainly neither Washington nor Moscow sought the advice of Seoul or Pyongyang about when and how the global cold war should be terminated. Even Tokyo, with its far greater geoeconomic clout, was barely consulted. Similarly China's stature did not grant Beijing a voice in this resolution. Asia was treated by the cold war's superpowers as an adjunct to the main theater; the Asia-Pacific region would simply have to react and adjust to events evolving among the main players. In many ways this perception by American leaders was warranted. It certainly conformed to the Atlanticist rules of the then existing game.

Nonetheless, a case can be made that Japan and the "little dragons" (including South Korea) played a central economic role in the West's broad-gauged pressures on the Soviet Union and the Warsaw Pact states. Given the economic anxiety expressed by the Euro-American portions of the broadly defined West regarding challenges from Asia's new centers of economic power, there is little doubt that Moscow & Co. were brought down by their noncompetitiveness measured against a Western economic coalition that encompassed Asia's advanced states. Consequently, a case can be made that South Korea played a real part in the economic processes of ending the cold war. South Korea's steadfastness as a U.S. ally also played a role, but it was so narrowly focused on North Korea that its significance vis-à-vis the Soviet Union and the Warsaw Pact states almost certainly was negligible. Against this background, was South Korea a player or a bystander as the cold war ended? It actually was both, but—because it is not widely credited with a players' role—it functioned primarily as a bystander.

Seoul was, however, an active bystander. Partly owing to foresight, but largely as a result of being in the right place at the right time with the right frame of mind, Seoul was well positioned to take advantage of opportunities created by the end of the cold war. Several trends converged to facilitate this situation. South Korea's economic successes, juxtaposed to North Korea's stagnation, opened new vistas for Seoul and decidedly tilted the diplomatic race the two halves of Korea had been engaged in toward the ROK. As part of that process South Korea's hosting the 1986 Asia Games and 1988 Olympics fostered a spirit and momentum that positioned Seoul for opportunities. In these terms, urged on by domestic political unrest that promised rewards for foreign policy successes that could deflect criticism, Seoul made its own luck. However, U.S.-USSR and European events beyond South Korean control loosed geopolitical forces precisely when Seoul was ready to seize the moment. This led to a rapid surge in ties between the ROK and the USSR and subsequently between the ROK, the Russian republic, and other elements of the former Soviet Union. In part because South Korea did not bear the historical baggage regarding Russians that the Japanese did, and in part because Seoul was more entrepreneurial in its diplomacy than Tokyo was, these efforts flourished in the late 1980s and early 1990s. Comparable changes occurred in ROK–People's Republic of China relations. The clear loser in these matters was North Korea. Pyongyang's world was collapsing around it as the cold war thawed.

These changes raise a key question about context in Korea. In one sense there was a dramatic change in the context of the Korean peninsula. The divided Korean nation saw its relationships with all the interested external players changed in fundamental ways. The relative power and clout of the two Koreas were similarly altered. In that setting the stresses influencing the gap between the two halves of a divided Korea were affected, which, in turn, reshaped the context in which options for Korean unification are raised. It also transformed the context in which the U.S.-ROK alliance discerns its identity. After all, the dichotomy between Seoul's primary focus on North Korea and Washington's primary focus on the Soviet Union, which was briefly accentuated in the late cold war years as South Korea moved toward the Soviet Union (to the consternation of some Americans), was eradicated by the collapse of the Soviet Union.

Against that background one could conclude that the end of the cold war dramatically changed for the better the circumstances behind the U.S.-ROK alliance and strengthened South Korea's hand in dealing with North Korea on unification. Despite those positive developments, however, Korea's version of the cold war has not ended and in some ways has intensified. North Korea's relatively greater isolation and its pursuit of a nuclear option underscore that hard reality. What is not clear is whether the Korean cold war is an anachronistic relic of *the* cold war or whether the Korean version always had a separate identity that has outlasted the U.S.-USSR version.

Evidence can be cited in support of both cases. Because the division of Korea predated the cold war and helped produce it, there has been a strain of separate identity throughout the cold war years that was reinforced by the indigenous animosities between North and South Korean leaders. That strain was strengthened by North Korea's idiosyncratic development of an ideology loosely based on Marxism but also drawing on deep-seated traditional Korean values.

There is no doubt, however, that the international cold war greatly influenced the course of Korea's cold war. Each half of Korea was reoriented toward its cold war backers. The divided Korean peninsula became a symbol of the main cold war, intensifying the difficulties of reunification. Despite the separate objectives of Washington and Seoul, the U.S.-ROK alliance became part of the Asian cornerstone of the United States' global alliance network.

The Crucial Transition Phase

Therefore, the post–cold war Korean situation is simultaneously an extension of unique circumstances and a relic of the cold war, which causes uncertainty about how Korean unification may be handled, how the U.S.-ROK alliance may evolve, and what a unified Korea might mean for the alliance relationship. (The alternative scenarios that might lead to Korean unification are intriguing, but this is not the place to explore them. As noted at the beginning of this chapter, it assumes that Korea shall be unified.) The point is that Korea's unification will end Korea's version of the cold war—whether one considers it as a generic or a specific phenomenon. Nonetheless, Korean unification and the end of its cold war will draw on the legacy of how South Korean leaders (who presumably will become the initial leaders of the unitary Korean state) and American leaders view the conditions that will have produced unification. Consequently, the forthcoming transition phase will be crucial in shaping the future of the United States' relations with a unified Korea—perhaps including an alliance.

For example, the financial costs of unifying Korea will influence the internal stability and viability of the resulting state. Were a unified Korea to be nearly bankrupted by the costs of unification, it might be more of a liability than an asset within a U.S.-Korean alliance. Unification might not be the boon that South Koreans hope it will be to the larger Korean economy's prospects. Instead, unification could severely set back the Korean economy, allowing other countries in Asia to progress while Korea does not. The societal impact of unification is the topic of another chapter in this volume, but it is important to note here the enormous potential for social disorder in Korea, for the difficult assimilation of two societies that have been more alienated from each other than Germany's *Ossies* and *Wessies,* and for tremendous disillusionment on the part of Koreans who discover that unification is no panacea for the problems caused by a divided nation's trauma. In turn, all those potential internal Korean ramifications pose enormous questions about the future desirability of Korea as an ally for the United States. These are all pessimistic possibilities. The future may prove to be more upbeat. Koreans may unify harmoniously, cheaply, and with no bitter aftertaste. But no one knows what will happen as the process unfolds, least of all Americans who assume the desirability of an alliance with a unified Korea. It behooves both sides to evaluate each other's utility as an ally after the process of unification clarifies the nature of the Korean state.

In the meantime each government must do what it can to prepare for unification. Probably the most important bilateral characteristic of the transition phase between the end of the global cold war and the forthcoming end of the Korean cold war is the extent to which Washington and Seoul are adjusting to changes and planning for a future that will include a unified Korea. To put it mildly, South Korea is far more prepared than the United States. Seoul has greater incentives, of course, because it is dealing with its own future. For Americans, prospective policy options regarding a unified Korea do not, and should not, occupy more than a small portion of the United States' international horizon. Nonetheless, it is unfortunate that South Korea is so far ahead in preparing for the end of its own cold war even as it copes with the realities imposed by the end of the global cold war. Americans are preoccupied with adjusting to the implications of the end of the global cold war for Asia. The United States is scarcely ready to devise an Asia-focused post–cold war policy—much less to prepare for what the end of Korea's cold war (and the reunification of Korea) will mean for the United States' still evolving post–cold war Asia policy.

To the extent the United States has planned for a postunification Korea, Washington is making what amounts to a straight-line projection about the continued need for U.S. armed forces within a U.S.-Korean alliance for the sake of Korean and regional stability. Behind these contemporary assumptions are U.S. concerns about the need to reassure Seoul about the United States' readiness to stay committed to its Korean allies as they try to cope with the short-run North Korean nuclear threat, the political and economic trauma that might occur as Korea unifies, and the problems associated with Japanese and Chinese options regarding a future unified Korea. These are all well-founded concerns, but it is not clear that they are well thought through or well explained to the American public. U.S. policy makers must carefully assess what Korean unification will mean before they proceed too far on the basis of assumptions about U.S. policy after Korea unifies. Americans (and our Japanese security partners) should methodically prepare for Korean unification. Among the questions that need answers are How fast will unification occur? Should we help accelerate the process (or hobble it)? What are the meaningful parallels (if any) with Germany's unification track record? Will Seoul expect Washington (and Tokyo) to help share the financial burdens of Korean unification? What proportions might that assistance assume? What kind of political leadership can we expect to see emerge from a unified Korea? What are the likely parameters of a unified Korea's foreign policy? What will its security interests be versus its neighbors—China, Japan, and Russia? How may Beijing, Tokyo, and Moscow perceive a unified Korean state and its policies toward them? What contingencies may a balance of power among China, Japan, Russia, and Korea portend for U.S. policy?

Relations with a Postunification Korean State

Not unless Americans can come up with reasonably solid answers to these questions should the United States overtly plan to extend the U.S. alliance to cover its relations with a postunification Korean state. To do otherwise is to buy the proverbial pig in a poke. In short, existing U.S. willingness to perpetuate the alliance involves unnecessary risks. If Americans reconsider this option, there are a number of salient factors to evaluate. Although the United States probably will continue to have an interest in Northeast Asian stability, it is not clear what the threats to that stability might be. One could argue that the Japan-Korea enmity is so endemic that the United States must remain as a strategic buffer between them in perpetuity or until they learn to love each other. Although there may be such a need by Koreans and Japanese, it is not clear why Americans should be willing to volunteer for what amounts to a difficult, permanent entangling alliance that mocks the wisdom of Presidents Washington and Jefferson. Of course, such a U.S. presence would continue to project U.S. influence in the region, and some will no doubt argue that this use of military power is essential for U.S. vital interests. This may be true, but it cannot be considered certain because Americans may discover that an economic projection of U.S. national presence is more important than a military projection in the region.

Beyond that larger issue, which will influence the overall tenor of American foreign policy, the United States needs to consider specific possibilities bearing on American relations with postunification Korea. What countries might pose a threat to Korea? The most likely candidates are Japan, China, and Russia. It is impossible to say for certain what U.S. interests may be vis-à-vis any of those countries an unknown number of years from now after Korea is unified, but it is not unreasonable to believe that any of them might outrank Korea on a hypothetical list of U.S. priorities. Why then should the United States be so confident today that it will want to wed itself to Korea's security in an unknown context? This is not to suggest that Korea might not be an excellent ally. For example, were the United States to perceive a threat from China against U.S.-Japan interests, or from Japan against U.S.-China interests, Korea could prove very useful. In this regard one should note the likely predisposition of a unified Korea to revert to close ties with its traditional "big brother"—China. Americans must bear this in mind as Washington tries to calculate the potential utility of Korea as a future strategic partner. Were a unified Korea to display antagonism toward a neighbor with which the United States has solid relations, however, there would be little reason for the United States to side with Korea against more important U.S. interests.

For example, during the cold war both China and Japan were pragmatic about the utility of a divided Korea for their respective national interests. It was (and is) a useful buffer state. In the late cold war and early post–cold war years, Korea's division also helped China and Japan keep the United States engaged militarily in Northeast Asia. In the 1990s China values that presence in Korea as a means to keep a lid on Japanese ambitions. In turn, Japan treats the U.S. military presence in Korea as a reinforced buffer between it and a China that might again display "Middle Kingdom" behavior. Tokyo also finds North Korea's role as a threat to be a useful surrogate for the former Soviet Union, helping Japan keep Americans interested in defending Asia from generic instability. A divided Korea has been (and is) useful to its neighbors for these reasons. In contrast, a unified Korea would play none of those geopolitical roles. Furthermore, Korean animosities toward Japan, which have been partially diffused by inter-Korean rivalries, could find free expression in a unified state. The possibility that a unified Korea would retain large armed forces inherited from its two predecessors cannot go unnoticed by its neighbors, especially Japan. Given past South Korean willingness to line up beside the United States and against Japan on trade and burden-sharing issues, it does not take much imagination for Tokyo to visualize a unified Korea as a source of new problems. Although those frictions might create opportunities for Beijing vis-à-vis its traditional "younger brother," they also would denote a new form of instability for China. As long as American relations with Japan or China or both are more important to Washington than U.S.-Korean ties, Americans should be cautious about prematurely embracing a unified Korean state as an ally without knowing the threats inherent in such an alliance.

In that light, Americans should consider the pressures likely to be on a unified Korean state. Even today one can see ample evidence that Seoul is pursuing an independent foreign policy, moving rapidly away from the remnants of its client-state past toward a more assertive (and less reactive) foreign policy style.[3] In that regard U.S.–South Korean ties are experiencing a healthy maturation process. Again assuming that Seoul will lead a unified Korea, it is reasonable to expect that this trend will continue after unification. In fact, it seems likely that the heady atmosphere of unification will accent Korean nationalistic fervor. In addition, Seoul would have to cope with what might be called the "repeninsularization" of Korea. Throughout the years of Korea's division—but especially after the Korean War—the two Koreas have been precluded from being a complete peninsula (*hando*, or half island) on the Asian continent. South Korea has functioned as a de facto full-fledged island (*do*), generating an islander's thinking about the need for allies, logistics, and a maritime context for the North-South Korean confrontation. As South Korea prospered and became a more valued partner for the United States, it increasingly became meshed into the United States' maritime orientation in the Pacific. For its part, North Korea devolved into half a peninsula (what could be called a *han-hando*). It was weakened by the "island" appended to its southern border that imposed serious strategic and economic obstacles.

When Korea reunifies, it will become a complete peninsula once more. It is possible that, after gaining control of the entire peninsula, Seoul will retain a large portion of its maritime thinking in order to work with the United States and Japan. However, it is also possible that the long tradition of Korean continentalism will reassert itself as Korea adjusts to being a peninsula jutting out from China. This could have a major impact on proposed plans for the continuation of the U.S.-Korean alliance into the post-unification era. Can the alliance be transformed from part of a maritime-oriented network into a maritime-continentalist hybrid? This might work for Korea but would draw the United States in strategic directions it has avoided for many years. It is uncertain whether Americans could acquiesce to these arrangements.

Aside from these primarily Korean considerations, the future of the U.S.-ROK alliance after Korean unification must also factor in narrowly American considerations. As one can see in Europe and elsewhere in Asia, the U.S. debate over a proper level of foreign commitment is far from resolved. The Clinton administration may be blazing a path toward a multilateralist new world order in harmony with mid-1993 statements by President Kim Young-sam and Foreign Minister Han Sung-joo about South Korea's interest in multilateral security.[4] Or, conversely, the Clinton administration may be moving toward the kinds of international roles visualized by political figures as diverse as Ross Perot, William Weld, Dick Gephardt, and Pat Buchanan, who almost certainly would lead the United States in different directions. In short, the United States faces a period of foreign and defense policy flux, and it is uncertain what may emerge.

One of America's foremost Asia specialists, Chalmers Johnson, has raised two innovative points that are relevant for future U.S.-Korean security ties. Although Johnson recommends removing U.S. ground forces from Korea, he suggests that a long-term alliance with Korea be maintained as a way to keep Japan and China a bit off balance. In turn, he sees the United States' somewhat strained relations with Japan and China as part of an emerging larger Asian balance of power supported by American ties with Korea, Vietnam, and the countries of the Association of Southeast Asian Nations.[5] This particular vision for a new U.S. policy in Asia is one of many that will compete for American popular support in the post–cold war years. Out of that competition will emerge a foreign policy designed for the new era by new people, which leaders of Korea (and other Asian countries) must address.

Similarly, and partially driving the first dynamic, the U.S. economy faces significant uncertainties. Neither Americans nor their current allies can be sure that the U.S. economy will sustain the levels of American international commitments to which they have all grown accustomed. High costs and frustrations over the murkiness of post–cold war purposes aggravate the economic underpinnings of U.S. commitments to its allies. These sentiments were forcefully expressed by Peter Tarnoff, third-ranking official in the Clinton State Department.[6] They caused quite a flap and were unconvincingly disavowed by Secretary of State Warren Christopher.[7] This controversy is symbolic of the debate over national capabilities and purposes occurring among Americans. All these, and perhaps other unforeseen, domestic American factors, are likely to shape U.S. policy generally, and toward Korea, in the coming years.

Against that cautionary note, it is safe to conclude that the prospects for the U.S.-Korean alliance are sound for the short term but are less certain over the longer term. When that longer term encompasses Korea's unification, the alliance's prospects will grow even less certain. There are too many unknowns waiting in the future for either Americans or Koreans in 1994 to confidently forecast that the alliance will be intact after Korea unifies in five, ten, fifteen, or fifty years. Moreover, Americans can do little more than guess what U.S. national interests vis-à-vis that unified Korean state might be. Whether one uses economic, strategic, political, or regional criteria, the potential variables are so numerous that it makes no sense to express positive certainties about the future. It is far wiser for both current allies to prepare plans based on a range of contingencies. These could readily include our current preference for continuing the alliance in some form, but prudence demands that the policy spectrum also incorporate mutual autonomy, new allies, and new coalitions. These may seem like broaching the unthinkable in the circumstances prevailing in 1994, but this step is necessary for the formulation of balanced policies by both allies, especially in light of Kim Il Sung's death.

Notes

1. For representative analyses of past Korean unification alternatives, see Bong-youn Choy, *A History of the Korean Unification Movement: Its Issues and Prospects* (Peoria, Ill.: Institute of International Studies, Bradley University, 1984); Tae-hwan Kwak, Chong-han Kim, and Hong-nack Kim, eds., *Korean Unification: New Perspectives and Approaches* (Seoul: Institute for Far Eastern Studies, Kyungnam University, 1984); John Sullivan and Roberta Foss, eds., *Two Koreas—One Future?* (Lanham, Md.: American Friends Service Committee and University Press of America, 1987); Tae-hwan Kwak, *In Search of Peace and Unification on the Korean Peninsula* (Seoul: Seoul Computer Press, 1986); Sang-woo Rhee, *Security and Unification of Korea* (Seoul: Seoul National University Press, 1978).

2. For example, see the views of Republic of Korea foreign minister Han Sung-joo in the *Korea Herald*, March 7, 1993, p. 2. The most explicit expression of that intent by the Clinton administration was then Deputy Secretary of Defense William J. Perry's comments during a visit to Japan in the *Korea Herald*, May 14, 1993, p. 1, and the *Los Angeles Times*, May 16, 1993, wire service.

3. An example of this was Seoul's exploration of ties with European weapons suppliers to compensate for what U.S. arms producers will not sell South Korea for fear that the technology transfer will make Korea too competitive. See the *Asian Wall Street Journal Weekly*, May 10, 1993, p. 4.

4. *Korea Herald*, May 25, 1993, pp. 1–2.

5. Chalmers Johnson, "Rethinking Our Asia Policy," *National Interest*, Summer 1993.

6. *Washington Post*, May 26, 1993, pp. A1 and A24.

7. Secretary Warren Christopher's interview on the "MacNeil-Lehrer News-Hour," Public Broadcasting System, June 1, 1993.

Contributors

NICHOLAS EBERSTADT is a visiting scholar at the American Enterprise Institute and a visiting fellow at the Harvard University Center for Population and Development Studies. His books include *The Poverty of Communism* (1988) and *Foreign Aid and American Purpose* (1989). He is coauthor, with Judith Banister, of *The Population of North Korea* (1992) and editor of *Fertility Decline in the Less Developed Countries* (1981). His book *Korea Approaches Reunification* is scheduled for publication in 1994.

AIDAN FOSTER-CARTER is senior lecturer in sociology and the director of the Korea Project at the University of Leeds, England. His most recent book is *Korea's Coming Reunification*. His essays and articles have appeared in academic journals and in the *Far Eastern Economic Review, Business Asia, Financial Times, Guardian,* and *Sunday Times*. Author of the quarterly *Country Report on North Korea* published by the Economist Intelligence Unit, he visited North Korea in 1986 and 1990 and has made seven trips to South Korea. He was educated at Oxford University and Hull University.

THOMAS H. HENRIKSEN is a senior fellow and associate director of the Hoover Institution. He has written and edited several books and numerous articles on revolution, political change, and foreign involvement in the Third World. More recently, he has embarked on studies of U.S. foreign policy, defense issues, and international affairs. His administrative responsibilities include developing Hoover's Korean Studies Program.

MAN WON JEE is president of the Institute for Social Development in the Republic of Korea. He was adjunct professor of operations research at the U.S. Naval Postgraduate School at Monterey, California, during 1987–1989 and research director in the Management Systems Improvement Department, Korea Institute for Defense Analyses, during 1980–1987. The author of many articles and two books on Korean military affairs, he holds a B.S. degree from the Korea Military Academy and M.S. and Ph.D. degrees from the U.S. Naval Postgraduate School.

TETSUYA KATAOKA is a senior research fellow at the Hoover Institution. He has written several books on East Asian affairs and U.S.-Japanese relations including, most recently, *The Making of a Constitution*. He holds a Ph.D. degree from the University of Chicago and was a professor of political science at Tsukuba University, Japan.

KYONGSOO LHO is professor of public administration in Seoul National University, Korea, and director of studies at the Korean Institute of International Studies. He was a visiting scholar at the Hoover Institution and a research associate at the Center for International Security and Arms Control at Stanford University. A graduate of Harvard University, he received a doctorate in international politics from Oxford University, England. He has written two books and many articles on the major powers and inter-Korean relations.

JONGRYN MO is a research fellow at the Hoover Institution and assistant professor of government and Asian studies at the University of Texas at Austin. He has written articles on economic and trade relations between the United States and Korea and the politics of electoral systems in Korea. He is coeditor of the book *Shaping a New Economic Relationship between Korea and the United States*. Mo graduated from Stanford University with a doctoral degree in business.

EDWARD A. OLSEN is professor of Asian studies, Department of National Security Affairs, Naval Postgraduate School, Monterey, California. He holds graduate degrees from the University of California at Berkeley and the American University. During 1975–1980 he served as Japan/Korea political analyst in the U.S. Department of State, Bureau of Intelligence and Research, Office of East Asia–Pacific Affairs. Olsen is the author of five books and many articles. His most recent volume on Korea is *U.S. Policy and the Two Koreas*.

Index